D1525746

On Mountains &
MOUNTAINEERS

by
Mikel Vause

Published by
Mountain N'Air Books
La Crescenta, CA

Published in the United States of America
by
Mountain N'Air Books, P.O.Box 12540, La Crescenta CA 91224
Phone (818) 951-4150

Cover photograph: Ang Temissa and Lhakpa Dorje on the Ama
Dablam's South Ridge. – Taken by Tom Frost.
All other photographs by Tom Frost.
Cover and book lay-out designed by Gilberto d'Urso.

Library of Congress Cataloging-in-Publication Data
Vause, Mikel, 1952-
    On mountains & mountaineers / by Mikel Vause, – 1st ed.
        p.   cm.
    Includes bibliographical references.
    Contents: Sir Leslie Stephen – Giusto Gervasutti – Geoffrey Winthrop
Young – Sir John Hunt – Maurice Herzog – Wood Wilson Sayre –
Doug Scott – Arlene Blum – David Roberts – Albert Frederick Mum-
mery.
    ISBN 1-879415-06-2 $12.95
    1. Mountaineer s –Biography. 2. Mountaineering – Psychological aspect.
I. Title: On mountains and mountaineers.
GV199.9.V38 1993
796.5'22– dc20   93-5216
                    CIP

ISBN:1-879415-06-2

On Mountains & Mountaineers

Forward 5

Acknowledgements 7

Introduction 9

Sir Leslie Stephen 21
    The Intrinsic Reward: 23

Giusto Gervasutti 29
    Meant For The Mountain: 31

Geoffrey Winthrop Young 37
    Escape From Convention: 39

Sir John Hunt 45
    The Quest Metaphor: 47

Maurice Herzog 53
    The Ultimate Bond: 55

Woodrow Wilson Sayre 63
    The Paradox of Aloneness: 65

Doug Scott 73
    To Adapt and to Survive: 75

Arlene Blum 83
    Reaffirmation of Life: 85

David Roberts 93
    The Irony of Existence: 95

Albert Fredrick Mummery 107
    Climbing as Education: 109

Forward

$\mathcal{M}$ountaineering has a wonderfully rich literature, perhaps the richest of any sporting activity. One of the reasons for this is undoubtedly that mountaineering is so much more than a sport. It can certainly become a way of life for many; it has a deep spiritual or mystic significance; and for all of us, to a greater or lesser degree, it becomes an exploration not just for the physical unknown but also of our psyches. This is well reflected in the personalities whom Mikel Vause has chosen in his intriguing study of a wide range of personality from different periods in the development of climbing. Through this we can gain a greater understanding of what draws us into the mountains.—**Chris Bonington, C.B.E.**

Acknowledgements

I wish to express my thanks and appreciation to all those who have provided help and shown support for this effort. In particular, I wish to thank my wife Janis for her constant encouragement and my children Kelly, Emily, Sarah, and Jared for their love and enthusiasm for what I do. My friends and professors Richard Carpenter and Howard McCord for their encouragement in my studies in mountain literature.

Thanks also goes to Chris Bonington for his criticism and his forward, to George Lowe for his insights, and to Tom Frost for the use of his photographs. I wish also to thank LaRee Keller for her careful typing of the final manuscript, Gene Sessions for his editorial work, and Carl Porter for his help with the bibliography. I owe special thanks to Gilberto d'Urso for his faith in this project and his many hours of editing and manuscript preparation. I am also in great debt to all those I have had the good fortune to climb with over the years, in particular: Bill McVaugh, Lee Schussman, Bruce Roghaar, Russ Burrows, Jock Glidden, Bob VanDyke, Paul Wilcox and Mike Lattin.—**Mikel Vause**

The Chamonix Aguilles

Introduction

*H*umans, in their search for knowledge and dominion, have struck out on many memorable expeditions to achieve these desires, many times at great risk. The old adage "Nothing ventured; nothing gained" summarizes the attitudes that rationalized the risk factor. But another element attached to the idea of risk was that there must be some purpose connected to the venture, i.e.: land, gold, science and personal fame. The idea of risk-taking for anything other than material gain or for science was sheer lunacy.

This is also clearly represented in other forms of activity that are risky such as Arctic exploration. Roald Amundsen, after being the first man to reach the South Pole, had little to show for it; he was greatly in debt and physically worn out. His only reward was the fact that he had done it.

The very birth of alpine climbing came as a result of an offer made by the Genevese scholar Horace-Benedict de Saussure, who, after first reviewing Mont Blanc in 1760, offered a reward to anyone who reached the summit. It is ironic that an activity that, in the late part of the present century, is practiced for intrinsic, almost solely spiritual reasons, was the child of materialism. Material motive no longer accounts for mountaineering, yet the encouragement of individuality and personal liberty, the sort of romantic freedom that led visionary humans to great achievements and rewards in science, industry, and exploration is still questioned when applied to mountaineering. This is possibly due to mountaineering being so purely visionary as well as so lacking in any material recompense. Robert Frost examines the idea of climbing for its own sake in his poem "The Mountain":

. . . It doesn't seem so much to climb a mountain
You've worked around on foot of all your life.
What would I do? Go in my overalls,
With a big stick, the same as when the cows
Haven't come down to the bar at milking time?
Or with a shotgun for a strong black bear?
Twouldn't seem real to climb for climbing it.
(*Lathem 40-44*)*

Even in a time of constant thrill-seeking and "adrenalin highs," the most adamant adventurer sees climbing as a sure-fire path to suicide. Those generally associated with mountain climbing are seen as somewhat deranged, having a death wish. In a television documentary dealing with the American Everest North Face Expedition, the American climber, Jim Wickwire, was asked why death seemed to override his wish to live, a question naturally directed to him as a mountaineer. His answer was that the death wish attributed to climbers is a fallacy, that in fact climbing is an affirmation of life and all of its goodness and joy.

The careful reading of essays dealing with ascent clearly illustrate that the climbers are more than just sportsmen, they are artists, poets, and philosophers. Like Emerson, Wordsworth and other great thinkers and poets who believed in the divine nature of humans, they reach their god-like potential through such challenges as those found climbing not only in the wild back country of the remote mountain ranges of the world, but many times in local crags as close to home as Walden Pond was to Thoreau's Concord.

Wilfrid Noyce, a prolific writer as well as active participant in mountaineering, states that the desire for risk and adventure is innate:

If adventure has a final and all-embracing motive, it is surely this:
we go out because it is our nature to go out, to climb mountains,
and to paddle rivers, to fly to the planets and plunge into the

---

* All citations in this text follow the M.L.A. Documentation style. For complete author and text information refer to the list of works cited, at the end of this book.

depths of the oceans . . . When man ceases to do these things, he is no longer man.(quoted in Schulthers 33)

But the climber must realize that with the commitment to climb comes responsibility and possibly death as a result of his choices.

An examination of the literature of mountaineering provides not only many exciting tales of high adventure, but also, if closely examined, one comes to understand the psychology and philosophy of those who wish, through the medium provided them by the ice-covered faces of nature's grand and timeless monuments, to ply their art in places of limited access. It is my intent to focus on the intellectual and social implications found in mountain writing as offshoots of the romantic essay rather than adventure stories only.

The literature of the mountains is transcendental by nature. Because language is limiting it contains the inevitably incomplete record of the climber/writer's sojourn in the ideal world, which though incomplete, still provides the reader with a vicarious account of enlightenment achieved by the climb, and a written vision of the climber's art achieved through his travels in the Earth's wild places and a record of the physical exhilaration felt by the climber fortunate enough to reach the summit. It matters not if it be a first ascent or the hundredth visit to the top, the experience is the end in itself.

The promise of reward to those willing to risk possible catastrophe is of little extrinsic value, but the intrinsic reward is beyond value or price. This gift from activity in wild nature is possibly best explained by John Muir who constantly sought after the prize found at the tops of mountains:

Climb the mountains and get their good tidings. Nature's peace will flow into you as sunshine flows into trees. The winds will blow their own freshness into you, and the storms their energy, while cares will drop off like autumn leaves. (Wolf, Unpublished Journals 317)

The mountaineer is glad for every opportunity to return to the mountains in search of the divinity only available to the hardy. Muir put into words the inner feeling of all climbers upon their return to the mountain wilderness:

I . . . am always glad

to touch the living rock again

and dip my head in the high mountain sky. (Wolf, Unpublished Journals 221)

This communion of humans with nature does not have to be unique to the climber, but to all who are willing to make the efforts needed—who willingly reach deeper within themselves to overcome the most difficult problems for the sake of the spiritual reward. In this study of writings which are the works of climbers, the purpose is to show that mountaineers are not only superb athletes, but also deep thinkers rather than demented and suicidal, and who, through their writing provide those who lack the climber's gift a record of the experience and possibly the understanding of the motives that drive the climber to scale the few high places and break from the otherwise natural horizontal existence of the generic human both literally and figuratively. The climber, by providing the record of his climb, acts as a proxy for those who, for various reasons are unable to go into the wilds. One philosophy of the mountaineer is very clearly presented by the Italian climber, Walter Bonatti, who explains the psyche of the climber as being set for high achievement, unwilling to settle for the mediocrity so commonly found in industrialized humans; who willingly takes risks, not for anything material, but for the uplift of the inner spirit which directs the character of humans in all of their aspects. This is not to say that the climber is a super human or semi-divine, but that their philosophical perspective is an explanation of why the climber undertakes such risks.

Bonatti refers again and again to the effects of industry on society and how humans have come gladly to settle for a mere fraction of their whole potential. He contrasts this dull, over-civilized humanoid with the climber whose rebellion directed against the morbid effects one sees in "collective society" is manifest in their willingness to risk their lives in order to issue their protest against such an anesthetized existence as if found in most human settlements. This philosophy is not unique to Bonatti but is patently romantic and could as easily be the words of Wordsworth who in his poem "The Old Cumberland Beggar" states his concern of how industry affects man.

Along with recognition of the romantic ideal that is clear in climbing philosophy it must be remembered that the rewards of the adventure do not come easy. Rob Schultheis explains the efforts of achieving spiritual growth by adventure this way:". . . Adventuring requires determination, curiosity, toughness, and—especially—the ability to solve problems with real creativity"(34), the same elements found anywhere there is success. It is with this in mind that the climber/writer writes.

All humans need to participate in adventure, to pioneer new frontiers, sometimes even at the risk of.life, and to do it under their own power using few and possibly none of technology's products to add an even greater feeling of accomplishment and contribute to their ascent—physically and spiritually.

The philosophy of unencumbered progress as advocated most clearly by Henry David Thoreau, in **WALDEN**, is also the philosophy of Walter Bonatti, who states that though climbing starts out as a sport, the end result can be great spiritual rewards, and that the less material baggage one takes into the mountains, the greater the possibility of reward.

Bonatti's belief is that mountaineering is an activity which provides inspiration and fulfills requirements set by his temperament, and which follows a tradition established "out of sacrifice, suffering and . . . love," which does not allow for the easy win or to win at any cost. Bonatti's philosophy fits the theory of risk exercise (RE) of Dr. Sol Ray Rosenthal, who after many years of research and study has found "that there is something in risk that enhances the life of the individual—something so real, something with such impact that people who've experienced it need to experience it again and again" (Furlons 40).

The idea of risk must be clarified; it is more than just "the joy of survival or a sense of self-validation. It [is] a powerful psychic and visceral kick—an exhilaration, a euphoria, a sense of heightened awareness" (Furlons 93).

Heightened consciousness is reward of the transcendental experience common to Emerson, Thoreau and Muir. Dr. Rosenthal indicates that such "transcendent" experiences are common to the risk taker. Risk taking results in a very personal revelation about one's limitations and abilities. What is "risky" to one may be commonplace to another, but regardless, "risk. . . heightens perceptions because it enforces an absolute concentration on the moment, as opposed to the ennui. This can pervade any endeavor in which there's nothing important at stake" (Furlons 94).

Dr. Rosenthal, in an interview with **OUTSIDE** magazine's William Berry Furlons, explains the differences between RE and risk taking this way: Risk exercise differs from the common concept of risk taking in that it is measured. Rosenthal is not talking about a mindless pursuit, such as diving off the Golden Gate Bridge to see if, just this once, you can survive. "In the manic risk, terror or despair is the only predictable emotion," he says. One of the assumptions of RE is that the risk taker has the skills to match or overcome the risk. "Otherwise terror simply overwhelms the RE response."

At the same time, however, the greatest RE response comes when the risk tests the skills of the risk taker. "It takes him up to the far frontier of his skills," says Rosenthal, "but it shouldn't take him mindlessly beyond it." He believes that a risk taker who goes rashly and repeatedly beyond his skills is seeking something other than an RE response.

In essence, this response is a sensation that envelops the risk taker, usually, though not inevitably, after the activity. The sensation varies in intensity and duration according to the individual and to the degree of risk. Rosenthal is careful to distinguish the RE response from the "adrenalin high" some risk takers say they have experienced. Adrenalin, notes Rosenthal, is simply a "fight or flight" secretion that speeds up the body or gives it more energy. The RE response goes further, taking on both a strong sensory and strong cerebral dimension.

Sensory: "In talking with people who've had an RE response," says Rosenthal, "you find that they describe a very pronounced sense of well-being. In most people it's a feeling of exhilaration, even euphoria. They talk of having achieved more of their potential as human beings, of feeling fulfilled and yet having a greater expectancy of their lives." They talk, he adds, not only of feeling keenly aware of the world around them, but also of themselves and their own awareness. They not only see, for example, but they know what they see. And they know that they know. This accounts for the risk taker's vivid feeling of potency—he can control his increased sensory power beyond anything he ever knew. Unlike someone who is drunk or otherwise mind-altered, he is not separated from reality. "Reality doesn't intimidate him, because he feels so good within himself," says Rosenthal. "He has the strong feeling that his whole life has been enhanced, that he has been enhanced."

Cerebral: In the more pronounced RE response, the individual enjoys the power and pleasure of summoning up the "wholeness" of his thought. His mind, given more information from his senses, somehow seems to give it all greater meaning. At the same time, the mind discriminates among the various sensations and meanings so that there is less mental clutter and an increased capacity for setting priorities. "The result is that people find their concentration is increased immensely," says Rosenthal. "They find that they can go to the heart of a problem and find a solution." What if the problem is emotional, not cerebral? "They manage to take the hardest step in meeting such a problem—they recognize that it involves their emotions, not their reason, which is an enormous discipline in itself."

For generations, risk activities were thought to be for the inane or the insane. "We've all been taught from infancy that danger, the presence of risk, is the signal to stop, to turn back, to cease whatever we're doing," says Rosenthal. People who persisted in risk taking were said to be unbalanced in a dazzling variety of ways. Some were said to have death wishes, the favorite cliche of journalism. Some were said to be exhibiting super-masculinity as a way of overcoming subconscious feelings of inadequacy. Some were said to be counterphobic, seeking to conquer their own worst fears by exposing themselves to whatever caused those fears. Rosenthal, on the other hand, believes that measured risk becomes understandable and even desirable when seen simply as the act of a person seeking to enhance his life by exploring inner resources. (Furlons 40-93)

Mountaineering, clearly, is more closely related to RE (risk exercise) than to risk taking, because its effects or rewards are mostly intrinsic.

The influence of mountaineering and the results of the influences are the creation of a more spiritual and ultimately responsible individual who is given over to the spiritual intrinsic betterment which comes from increased personal awareness and self control in all situations rather than a self indulgent, self-centered being who receives uplift only through ratification of worldly appetites achievable by no effort or at best the slight effort it takes to unloose his purse strings.

The comparison made by Galen Rowell in his essay "Storming A Myth" dealing with the physical and spiritual explains in elegant terms the necessary philosophical approach to climbing:

I know that climbing is merely a vehicle, a tool, and the climber a tool user. As a tool, climbing can be used to over-come 5.12 cracks, the difficulties of a Grade 6 wall, or an 8000 meter peak. But held only to this narrow definition, it can eventually bring boredom and despair.

The climbing tool has a spiritual component as well. At the heart of the climbing experience is a constant state of optimistic expectation, and when that state is absent, there is no reason to continue climbing. "I have found it!" can apply not only to those who feel they have found God, but to those who, like me, continue to find Shangri-Las where we experience fresh, child-like joy in everything that surrounds us, including memories that are the most long-lasting and intense of our lives. (Tobias, **Mt. Spirit** 85-91)

It is the purpose of climber\writers to provide the reader with at least some information that was uplifting to them during the climb and which not only provides extrinsic justification for climbing, but also is an intrinsic reward, that comes from sharing their experiences with others. No matter how eloquent or profound writer are they cannot live the total experience for the readers, but through their writing they can entice the reader to an active involvement, possibly on a first-hand level. This tactic was used, with great effect, by John Muir during his campaign for national parks in America. His glowing reports of America's wild places attracted a great deal of attention. He invited all "over-civilized" people into the wilderness and promised them "terrestrial manifestations of God." Because of his writings many national parks were established like Yellowstone and Yosemite.

Doug Scott is a leader in modern British climbing and an active climber\writer. His essay, "On the Profundity Trail," an account of his climb of El Capitan's Salathe Wall with Peter Habeler, carries the idea of participation and calculated risk to the more limited audience of the climbers but is applicable to non-climbers as well and again illustrates Bonatti's mention of the harmful effects a collective society can have on man.

Not only does Scott support Bonatti's basic philosophy, but his ideas also tie in with the Emersonian theory of the transcendental experience from contact with wilderness. This results in personal growth as well as a "higher conduct of life" when one returns to the social world. But according to Scott the chances of achieving such spiritual and intellectual heights come from one's willingness to risk something of value—the longer the trip the more risk involved and the greater the possibility of growth.

These examples represent the psychological and philosophical ideas that help connect the realities of mountaineering, mountains, and travel. The next step is to see the effects mountains have had on literature. One can hardly read the works of the romantic writers, regardless of nationality, without coming across numerous references to mountains or wild terrain: man being naturally impelled to ascent in all its forms. This literature could hardly exist without reference to mountains and attempts to ascend them. As before mentioned, after man put aside the need for justification for climbing mountains, i.e. science and material wealth, mountains become a source of spiritual riches. The effort made to climb them was rewarded by spiritual uplift and a triumph of the inner man over himself. Samuel Taylor Coleridge, in 1802, made what has been recorded as the first descent of Scafell Cliff in the lake district of England. Just the small entry in his notebooks that recorded the event is filled with awe and wonder: "But O Scafell, thy enormous Precipices." The description of Coleridge's climb appears under the dates of August 1 and 9, 1802:

> The poet Samuel T. Coleridge made what he described as a "circumcursion" from Keswick by Newlands to Buttermere and St. Bees, up Ennerdale, thence by Gosforth to Wasdalehead, from where he climbed Scafell, descended to Taws in Eskdale, and then continued by Ulphaand, Coniston to Brathay and so back to Keswick. It is clear from his notebooks, now in the British Museum, that he descended from the summit of Scafell to Mickledore by the route we now call Broad Stand. He got down by "dropping" by the hands over a series of "smooth perpendicular rock" walls, got "cragfast" or nearly so, and finally slid down by a "chasm" or "rent" as between two walls. He recorded too that on reaching Mickledore his "limbs were all of a tremble," a phenomenon not unknown among modern cragsmen. (*Mountain* 30:17-18)

It was sixty years before the next climb of Scafell was recorded.

The myth of mountains being terrible and the hiding places of evil was dispelled by the men who climbed and returned with a report of the sublime rather than dread. As John Ruskin explained:

Thus the threatening ranges of dark mountains, which in nearly all ages of the world, men have looked upon with aversion or with terror, are in reality sources of life and happiness far fuller and more beautiful than the bright fruitfulness of the plain. (Smith **Armchair Mountaineer** 182)

Lord Byron, in his poem "Solitary," written in 1820, takes the idea of Ruskin further: To climb the trackless mountains all unseen, the wild flock that never needs a fold, alone o'er steeps and foaming falls to lean, This is not solitude; 'tis but to hold Converse the Nature's charms, and view her stores unrolled. (Styles 337)

Byron in "Solitary" mentions the extrinsic beauties of the mountains but in "The True Shrine" he explains the intrinsic blessing derived from mountains by those who climb them:

Not vainly did the early
Persian make
His alter the high places and
The peak
Of earth-o'er gazing mountain,
And thus take
A fit and unwalled temple,
There to seek
The Spirit, in whose honour shrines
Are weak,
Upreared of human hands.

The awesome power of nature is also recorded by Wordsworth in his poem "England and Switzerland, 1802" in which he deals with the sea and the mountains and the freedom that wild places provide for the man who is willing to venture out:

Two voices are there; one is of the sea,
One of the mountains, each a mighty voice;
In both from age to age thou didst rejoice,
They were the chosen music, Liberty!
There came a tyrant, and with holy glee
Thou fought'st against him—but hast vainly striven:

Though from thy Alpine hides at length and riven
Where not a torrent murmurs heard by these.
—Of one deep bliss thine ear hath been bereft;
Then cleve, O cleve to that which still is left—
For high—soul'd maid, what sorrow would it be
That Mountain floods should thunder as before,
And Ocean bellow from the rocky shore,
And neither awful Voice be heard by Thee!

As early as 1668 William Penn recognized the virtues and necessity of wild nature even from a religious point of view:

Christ loved and chose to frequent Mountains, Gardens, Seasides. They are requisite to the growth of piety; and I reverence the virtue that feels and uses it, wishing there were more of it in the world. (Styles 157)

As mentioned before man seeks ascent; whether viewed from an evolutionary perspective or a religious perspective the need to move up is there. The whole society of man is built on advancement. In 1740 Alexander Pope talked of the inborn need for man to ascend, in the lines of his poem "Alps on Alps":

So pleas'd at first, the tow'ring Alps we try,
Mount o'er the vales and seem to touch the sky;
The eternal snows appear already past,
And the first clouds and mountains seem the last,
But those attain'd, we tremble to survey
The growing labours of the lengthening way;
Th' increasing prospect tires our wond'ring eyes—
Hills peep o'er hills, and Alps on Alps arise!

Even in times of sorrow and tragedy directly resultant from climbing the mountains there comes intrinsic beauty. In 1903 three climbers were killed while attempting to climb Coleridge's Scafell Cliff. Here is the epitaph from the gravestone in Wasdale Head church yard:

One moment stood they as the angels stand
High in the stainless immanence of air;
The next they were not, to their Fatherland
Translated unaware. (Styles 165)

The number of references to the grandeur and beauty, the strength and power, and the spiritual necessity derived from mountain travel are many. And many of the poetic lines are direct results of first hand experience of the poets in the mountains; but the writings of those who live to climb and participated in the ascents of the extremely high and wild mountains provide even better insight into the need to climb—for man to continually scrape and pull themselves toward the clouds by way of the eternal rocks and snow and ice of which the mountains are made.

Basically, it is a romantic tendency: this emphasis on individuality, on close contact with nature as a spiritual matter, on the release and freedom that comes from this kind of experience. And all this tends to be put in an elevated language, a kind of inspirational "chant." The selections also produce elevated ideas which are the result of serious craftmanship not as mountaineers only, but as artists, as writers.

As Hilair Belloc said: The greater mountains, wherein sublimity so much excels our daily things, that in their presence experience dissolves, and we seem to enter upon a kind of eternity. (Styles 153)

The next logical step in the evolution of mountain literature is the essay. Mountaineers have the distinction of being prolific writers. Some claim it is ego that stimulates such outpouring, but Emerson's "chant" theory appears to be a more correct conclusion as to why climbers write. Of all the many activities defined as sport, mountaineers and explorers have produced a larger canon than other groups of sportsmen. This may be partly due to the nature of the participants i.e., scholars, scientists, philosophers, clergy. All of them are required by virtue of their vocations to write, so it appears natural that they would also record and make observations about their avocations.

Sir Leslie Stephen

*L*eslie Stephen was born in London, England, in 1832, the son of Sir James Stephen, professor of modern history at Cambridge University.

He was educated at Eton, King's College School and Cambridge, graduating twentieth wrangler in 1854. Elected to a fellowship at Trinity Hall, he studied mathematics, became a lecturer and was ordained. Over the years, he modified his theological views to such a great extent that he eventually ceased to consider himself a clergyman. In 1864 Stephen settled in London, occupying himself by writing for the *Saturday Review* and *Pall Mall Gazette*. In 1871 he became editor of *Cornhill Magazine*. Stephen's next project became the editing of the *Dictionary of National Bibliography* which began in 1882.

Stephen's personal bibliography is very impressive. In addition to his contributions to the *Dictionary of National Bibliography* he published numerous articles in the **British Alpine Journal** and **Cornhill**. Stephen was known to the world through his articles on mountaineering long before his recognition as a critic and philosophical scholar.

His books are as follows: *Sketches of Cambridge, by a Don, The Playground of Europe, Science of Ethics, History of English Thought in the Eighteenth Century, The English Utilitarians*. Stephen also wrote short biographies of Gibbon, George Eliot, Pope, Johnson and Hobbes.

In 1867 Stephen married the daughter of William Makepeace Thackeray. She died eight years later. He then wed the widow of

Mr. Herbert Duckworth, a marriage that ended with her death in 1895. Both unions were of perfect happiness. His daughter from his second marriage is Virginia Woolf.

Stephen's climbing career began about 1858. His list of climbing achievements are as impressive as his literary ones. No one of his period showed more interest in mountaineering than did Stephen, as his record attests: first ascent of the Monte della Disgrazia, Passage of the Jungfrau Joch and Viescher Joch, first ascent of the Bietschhorn and Blumlis alp, Lyskamm from the west, first ascent of Rothhorn, Jungfrau from Lauterbrunen and Scher Pass, Col des Hirondelles, first ascent of Schreckhorn and first ascent of Mont Mallet. His climbing activity stopped around 1871 at the request of his wife. He was president of the Alpine Club from 1865 to 1868.

The Intrinsic Reward:

by Sir Leslie Stevens

"Regrets of a Mountaineer" represents a retrospective look at mountaineering by a former practitioner who, like the Landor of "Yes I write verses," watches from a distance with envy of the exploits of the younger generation.

Stephen mentions in his essay most, if not all, the theories modern psychology has attached to high-risk activities—to the eyes of the scientist or researcher Stephen accurately describes the feelings of wandering the high ridges of the wild places of Europe. It is his psychological insight as well as his philosophical understanding that makes this essay of literary importance. Stephen looked at the mountain as a symbol—one only fully understood through actual contact—first-hand experience. Much like Virginia Woolf's somewhat biographical character Professor Ramsey in *To the Lighthouse*, Stephen is somewhat amazed at the observations of those people who never venture into the mountains and then minimize their reality.

Stephen, after some introductory remarks on the vanished pleasures of cricket and rowing, brings up the particular loss he feels at no longer climbing the Alps. He alludes to those who think such feelings must be a mere affectation, while others place them on the level of climbing a greased pole. He relates the arguments which these critics present and then answers that mountaineering is a sport, like cricket or rowing. He also has fault to find with those who describe this sport in over poetical terms or derogate it by stressing its hardships. But for him there are impressions that go far beyond either of these ways of describing mountaineering.

Stephen is much like Dr. George Sheehan, cardiologist and marathon runner, who in his book *Running and Being* states even if medical science were to find running to be a serious health risk he would continue to run. He justifies this attitude on intrinsic grounds: the spiritual euphoria of physical exercise. This concept of necessary experience is for Stephen an allegory for his very existence. In order to pass judgement on any activity, place or person one must first experience their experiences—at least relatively so. His experience as both participant and observer of risk activity gives him a unique platform from which to analyze the reasons—the drives which push human beings to such sports—sports that "brings one into contact with the sublimest aspects of nature. . . to absorb and be penetrated by their influence" (Stephen 31).

He recognizes the "horizontal point of view" in mountaineering's critics that raises question and amazement to why anyone would leave the relative comfort and safety for home and family to risk both life and limb on the frozen reaches of some isolated peak for no other reason than the normal rewards of the adventurer which are intrinsic, spiritual in nature. Stephen turns to poetic lyricism very similar to the flowery enticements used by John Muir in America to encourage his readers to visit America's wild places if not physically, at least spiritually, and throw their support behind his conservation philosophy. This same intention of support and acceptance seems to be clearly what Stephen has in mind by his use of description as justification for his good experiences in the mountains: "I am standing at the foot of what, to my mind, is the most glorious of all Alpine wonders—the huge Oberland precipice, on the slopes of the Faulhorn of the Wengern Alp." (Stephen 33)

These lyric descriptions serve a second purpose that may also allow Stephen to argue against blind conclusions regarding mountains and mountaineers on the grounds of limited perspective. He maintains that all men live by attaching symbolic value to both concrete and abstract objectives. A mountain, like a flower garden, is obviously something tangible—dangerously so, but in the eyes of the mountaineer represents something spiritual, beautiful and alive just as the flower garden represents life and beauty to the city dweller. Stephen maintains that man's pitting himself against something dangerous, like a mountain or river

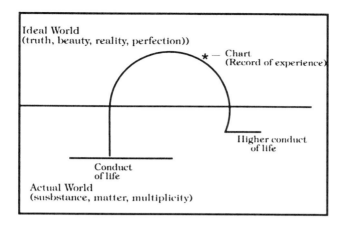

Ideal World
(truth, beauty, reality, perfection))

* — Chart
(Record of experience)

Higher conduct
of life

Conduct
of life

Actual World
(susbstance, matter, multiplicity)

or unexplored jungle though he may never reach the top still brings
an intrinsic reward that has lifted his confidence in himself as well as
his fellows upon his return to the mundane world. Doug Scott, a 20th
century mountaineer, recognizes the same outcome in his essay "On
The Profundity Trail." Both Stephen's and Scott's reaction is romantic,
clearly illustrated by Emerson's transcendental theories of Pragmatic
Mysticism. Emerson's idea is most clearly understood as illustrated in
graph form

IDEAL WORLD, truth, beauty, perfection

(Chant)
Higher Conduct of Life
Conduct of Life
ACTUAL WORLD: substance, matter, multiplicity
(Chant: Imperfect record of experience)

Emerson's theory (granted it is American, but is in harmony with,
and best illustrates the romantic philosophy whether British or American) is basically that man, by his entrance into wilderness, is taking
himself closer to the ideal realm of imagination, truth and reality. Although his stay is only temporary, like the climber's on the summit,
he returns to the world of his fellows with new light and knowledge.
His record of the experience comes in some artistic form—the "Chant"

is inaccurate but contains truth and serves as a message bearer to his fellows and raises the climber poet's conduct of life.

The spiritual record—the "Chant"—is not something that comes upon mere contact with mountains, but like every other worthy reward is the result of hard physical labor. Stephen makes it clear that the steepness of a snow-covered ridge, the ominous shadows of ice-covered vertical north faces, can only be overcome with the deepest, most strenuous physical effort:

> To him, perhaps, they recall the memory of a toilsome ascent, the sun beating on his head for five or six hours, the snow returning the glare with still more parching effect; a stalwart guide toiling all the weary time, cutting steps in hard blue ice, the fragments hissing and spinning down the long straight grooves in the frozen snow till they lost themselves in the yawning chasm below; and step after step taken along the slippery staircase, till at length he triumphantly sprang upon the summit of the tremendous wall that no human foot had scaled before. (Stephen 38)

To the non-climber this fact must first be recognized, after which the true elements of mountain beauty can be understood. These are the first two basic elements needed to recognize and appreciate the artistic product of the mountain experience:

One element of mountain beauty is their vast size and steepness. That a mountain is very large, and is faced by perpendicular walls of rock, is the first things which strikes the observer, and is the whole essence and outcome of a vast quantity of poetical description. Hence the first condition towards a due appreciation of mountain scenery is that these qualities should be impressed upon the imagination. The mere dry statement that a mountain is so many feet in vertical height above the sea, and contains so many tons of granite, is nothing. Mont Blanc is about three miles high (Stephen 34).

Writers like Henry James, James Joyce and Virginia Woolf maintain that life has no real meaning until it is placed in artistic terms. To the mountaineer, overhanging cliffs, yawning crevasses, and massive waterfalls become the artistic elements that make the mountain an artistic masterpiece in the eyes of the mountaineer and are the very things that make the climber want to see and touch them first-hand and for which they are willing to suffer physically, sometimes risking the possibility of death, to do so. The beauty of the mountains then becomes real and all-encompassing truth, whereas to the visitor to the valley who looks up at the mountains with no idea of their real size and magnitude can see only superficial beauty. Stephen clearly illustrates this:

> I do not say that the difference is quite so great in the case of the mountains; still I am certain that no one can decipher the natural writing on the face of a snow-slope or a precipice who has not wandered amongst their recesses, and learnt by slow experience what is indicated by marks which an ignorant observer would scarcely notice. . . . Hence I say that the qualities which strike every sensitive observer are impressed upon the mountaineer with tenfold force and intensity. If he is as accessible to poetical influences as his neighbors—and I don't know why he should be less so—he has opened new avenues of access between the scenery and his mind. (Stephen 40-43)

By way of contrast and realization, Stephen is not blind to the fact that even things as powerful and massive sometimes fail to influence certain climber's spirits:

> I have known some stupid and unpoetical mountaineers . . . who "do" the Alps; who look upon the lake of Lucerne as one more task ticked off from their memorandum book, and count up the list of summits visible from the Gornergrat without being penetrated with any keen sense of sublimity. (Stephen 44)

A climber must depart on the expedition with his priorities in line and thus be open to the real reason for venturing into the mountains: that of intrinsic reward and spiritual growth—the direct result of the physical challenge in wild surroundings and the fact that such rewards are worth risking everything including life to attain:

> Thus every traveller has occasionally done a sunrise, and a more lamentable proceeding than the ordinary view of a sunrise can hardly be imagined. You are cold, miserable, breakfastless; have risen shivering from a warm bed, and in your heart long only to creep into bed again. To the mountaineer all this is changed. He is beginning a day full of the anticipation of a pleasant excitement. He has, perhaps, been waiting anxiously for fine weather, to try conclusions with some huge giant not yet scaled. He moves out

with something of the feeling with which a soldier goes to the assault of a fortress, but without the same probability of coming home in fragments; the danger is trifling enough to be merely exhilatory, and to give a pleasant tension to the nerves; his muscles feel firm and springy, and his stomach—no small advantage to the enjoyment of scenery—is in excellent order. (Stephen 45)

The over-arching and undergirding philosophy of Stephen's essay is "to show that the mountaineer may boast of some intellectual pleasures; that he is not a scrambler, but that he looks for poetical impressions" (Stephen 56). These "poetic impressions" are inaccurate as stated in Emerson's theory because they are "beyond the power of art to imitate. . . [yet] may have a marvelously stimulating effect on the imagination.

GIUSTO GERVASUTTI

*G*iusto Gervasutti was the premier Italian Alpinist of pre-World War II. He was respected for his sense of dedication, physical condition, his sensitivity and self discipline. He was always pushing himself to higher standards as is clear with his list of climbing achievements: Matterhorn, solo, in winter; North Face of the Grandes Jorasses, Freney Piller Mont Blanc. His career was cut short by an accident while descending a new route on Mont Blanc da Tacul, which is now called the Gervasutti Pillar.

Gervasutti looked to the Great British climber A.F. Mummery as his mentor and much of Gervasutti's philosophy is reflective of Mummery's.

Giusto Gervasutti was born in 1909 and died in 1946. He published two books, *Alpinismo*, in 1935, which he co-authored with his climbing partner Rene Chabod and *Gervasutti's Climbs*. Gervasutti was possibly the last of the classic mountaineers coming from the golden age.

The last chapter in *Gervasutti's Climbs* is entitled "Conclusion," which is fitting, as herein is found the wisdom and philosophy of one, who because of his activity, has the strong knowledge of his past which allows him a far clearer vision of the future. One quality of much good literature is that it provokes not only thought but action. With the artistic skill of a story teller, Gervasutti in this essay, provides the reader with vision and foresight that has come down with him from the summits of the Earth's great mountains.

John Harlin at the top "Le Aguilles du Fau" 1963

Giusto Gervasutti

Meant For The Mountain:

Giusto Gervasutti

Giusto Gervasutti is unique in that he represents the classical tradition of mountaineering as it existed in the "Golden Age" in a world caught up in technical advancement. This is clear by his description of his taking only a rope to be used solely as a means of descent rather than a means of protection during the ascent. This presents an interesting picture of a man playing by the rules of the previous generation—a generation climbing for the spiritual rewards negating "those evil humours accumulated during the long monotonous hours of city life," rewards which enable him "to find serenity and calm in the freedom and exhilaration of climbing on difficult rock, in long silent communion with the sun, the wind, the blue sky, in the nostalgic sweetness of the sunset" *(Gervasutti 1-2)*. This type of mental and physical freedom, according to Gervasutti, is not found only in the excessive risks of solo climbing, or dogged chasing of summits. Neither is it found by one encumbered by new tools provided by technology, but is only found in man's spirit and psyche as it soars to heights of the imagination through physical and mental struggles found in the vertical world of the mountains. Many of today look at climbers as an unbalanced group of extremists, who for various reasons, seek total alienation from others of their kind by retreating to dangerously high and steep places not meant for the human animal, for such places are cold and silent. Climbing roped together is bad enough, but climbing solo, without rope or protection is worse yet—even suicidal. This public opinion toward climbers has changed little, for the attitude today is the same as in Gervasutti's time:

The popular view of solitary climbing is that it is simply a form of suicidal mania; and that the individual has no right to devote himself or his own free will to a sport involving excessive risks. (Gervasutti 69)

Gervasutti, like the great solo climbers of today like Messner, who soloed Everest without oxygen, or John Long or John Bacher, who climbed the great walls of Yosemite with nothing more than running shorts and climbing shoes, is not seeking death, but is enhancing life through the challenge of walking life's "less traveled roads."

It is the artist who seeks to express creativity through self expression, which is what the climber does; only the climber's expression is twofold. First the climber plies his art by actually climbing—at first by imitating those who went before, then by finding new, more challenging routes—not always more challenging because of technical difficulty but sometimes simply because they are unknown—untested. After the climb comes the "chant," the record of the adventure. The climber/writer tries as best he can to record the experiences of the climb—both physical and spiritual—the poetry of the climb. Both forms of expression are extremely difficult and require a great deal of discipline and creativity. In the actual climb this creativity is reflected in the craft of the practitioner, i.e. route finding, judgement of time, use or non-use of tools. In recording the climb it is to find the right words, phrases, metaphors to make it live, and always the written art falls short of the physical art. Percy Shelley in his "A Defense of Poetry" said "the most glorious poetry that has even been communicated to the world is probably a feeble shadow of the original conception of the poet"(Shelley 1109). Gervasutti reaffirms Shelley's theory when it comes to recording the climb because of the intensity of the actual experience:

The first is generally considered the superior; but to be able to endow pure thought with a value, one must be a poet and an artist. Only those who have attained to poetry can allow themselves the luxury of giving a universal value to the creations of their imagination, while remaining comfortably in their armchairs. But the others, and among them mountaineers, if they do not wish to limit themselves to the pleasures of imagination, must seek the satisfaction of their spirit's needs in action, and this satisfaction will be greater, and more complete, in proportion to the intensity of the action. (Gervasutti 76)

This perspective is corroborated by Doug Scott, one of Britain's greatest, and still active climbers who, in his essay "On the Profundity Trail," says:

If big wall climbing is pursued in a more hostile environment and for longer periods, of it the big wall climbers climbs alone, as Bonatti [and Gervasutti] did on the Dru then the doors of perception will open wide. The climbers involved may experience a more lasting state of heightened awareness, and may even reach a truly visionary, if not mystical state of being which transcends normal human comprehension. (12-17)

Yet Gervasutti's skill with words, like his skill in the mountains, shows through in his ability to express his philosophy so as to excite the reader with, at least, a fraction of his euphoria. His art of metaphor makes written experience come alive. In part of his essay Gervasutti is a bit critical of Paul Preuss, the great Austrian climber, who doggedly sought summits and who climbing alone was "betrayed by a treacherous hold, fell to his death." Yet with this knowledge so aptly expressed to his readers, Gervasutti still would strike out on his own "and no softer or more passive view of life could make me change my mind" (Gervasutti 70).

Gervasutti has the ability to express his feelings with lyric descriptions, beautiful enough to entice the most sedentary reader from his arm chair into activity:

He looked a bit dubious and stopped a minute to watch while I started slowly up. After wandering for a while among the pines and on the higher pastures, taking twice the normal time, I knocked at the door of the hut at two in the morning, drank two steaming grogs, and then lay down fully dressed on one of the bunks to rest for a couple of hours.

I left the hut at dawn. As the slope grew steeper I made my way up lightly with the cool mountain air giving me that delicious sensation of floating. My body was tingling with a wonderful sense of well-being, and ready to rise to whatever demands I made on it. (Gervasutti 71)

Within this lyricism Gervasutti recognizes the physical euphoria that medical researchers term as "Runner's High" that comes about during hard, distance runs which, due to chemicals called endorphins released by the body, pain is pushed aside and a "sensation of floating" is created. The same sensation Gervasutti experiences on a steep slope in "the cool mountain air."

To Gervasutti man was naturally meant to be in the mountains because man is made from the same elements. The Judeo/Christian explanation of man's physical makeup "from dust thou art and to dust thou shalt return" is reflected in Gervasutti's metaphor "I touched the rock with my hand almost stroking it, as one strokes something one loves but has not seen for some time." It is as if, because of the actual physical relationship with rocks—chemical make up, that man should commune with them. As Gaston Rebuffat said in **Starlight and Storm** "that's what we are made for" (119).

Why else would humans seek a relationship with a mountain? For the uplift of his spirit! The spiritual uplift (the transcendent experience) that clears away fear is clearly apparent in Gervasutti's explanation of a near fall on his solo climb of an unknown peak in the Dolomites, knowing full well the possible consequences of his undertaking:

Everything round me was quiet, with the rather startled silence of high places. I rubbed my foot two or three times on a polished bit of rock, as though to test its adherence, then I raised my arms in search of holds for my hands and, bracing my muscles, began to climb. I moved very slowly, without the least hurry, quietly looking for holds, studying each move so as to economize effort to the full. When a climber is on his own he can't afford to make the slightest mistake, for if he does, there is neither rope nor piton to save him. If his nerve goes, there is no friend to encourage him. And if danger suddenly strikes, all he can do is to risk everything; but if he loses, it is his life that is forfeit. (Gervasutti 72)

The intensity of actual experience as a means to reaching physical and spiritual as well as imaginative heights is clearly illustrated by Gervasutti's example of a near death experience in which he recognizes the literal possibilities of physical death:

I tried in every direction but it was no good. Although my feet did come in contact with the rock, I couldn't find the holds. I realized then that if I did not get up at once, all was over; the drop to the scree was getting on for 1,000 feet. (Gervasutti 73)

Obviously Gervasutti did not die, as he recorded his adventure, and this experience is not unique to Gervasutti, but is easily compared with John Muir's solo attempt of Mt. Ritter where he experienced the identical complications here described by Gervasutti, as did John Long on his solo of El Capitan detailed by Rich Ridgeway in **Outside** Magazine, January 1981:

Fifteen hundred feet off the ground on the East Buttress of Yosemite's El Capitan, John Long is as close as he has ever been to dying. He is climbing a crackless granite wall, ascending on small protrusions from an otherwise blank face. His hand is smeared on a smooth hold, and as he moves up he feels his fingers slipping. He has no pitons, no carabineers, no wedges or chocks or any of the paraphernalia climbers use to protect themselves should they fall. He had no rope.

Long is practicing what to rock climbers is the consummate expression of their art, and the consummate risk; free soloing. He has absolutely no latitude for error, and he knows further hesitation will be fatal. He tries to force any thoughts of falling from his mind; his fingers barely reach another tiny hold. He pulls, inching up, and reaches one more knob. Another move and he grabs the edge of a secure ledge.

Long is safe now. He sits back to rest, but realizing just how close he has come, he starts shaking violently. It takes a half-hour of meditative, rhythmic breathing before he has the composure to continue the climb.(34-35)

Yet even with death coming so close each man would obviously want to re-experience it. Why?

The grey mountain was indifferent. The valley floor was green and peaceful. Even the wind had died down. It was I, and I alone, who had sought this moment of suspense, created it, compelled it. Everything round me was motionless and static, had played no active part. And again the question surged up; "Why?"

No answer came—perhaps it never would. But when I reached the sun-flooded summit, with waves of floating mist beneath me, my heart sang for joy. The exaltation of that moment, out of the world, on the glory of the heights, would be justification enough for any rashness. (Gervasutti 74)

In the material oriented society in which we live it is indeed difficult to justify such behavior, but it is equally difficult to explain to a corporation why man needs to read poetry. Why risk your life when risk can be had in investing money, by playing the stock market or by investing in real estate. Humans are not meant to live non-physical lives. Their make up is to be active even if technology is making it convenient not to be. Humans must live heroically to reaffirm the freedom of the spirit, maintain the body, stimulate the intellect and satisfy the adventure instinct:

"Dare all, and you will be kin to the gods." (Gervasutti 77)

Geoffrey Winthrop Young

(1876-1958)

G. W. Young was, for years, the leading figure in British mountaineering. He was the son of Sir George Young who was responsible for the first ascent of the Jungfrau from Wengern Alp. Geoffrey's climbing career began with hill walks in Wales. As an undergraduate he began serious rock climbing in the Lake District of England. When unable to travel to the Lakes he climbed the spires around Trinity College. In 1900 he wrote *The Roof Climber's Guide to Trinity*. Young's serious climbs began shortly after 1900 with trips to the Oberland and Pennine Alps. In 1905 he teamed up with Joseph Knubel who was a professional guide. Together they climbed:

Weisshorn, South East Face

Taschorn, South West Face

Breithorn, Younggrat (Young's Ridge)

Dom, South West Face

Zinal Rothorn, East Face

Weisshorn, Younggrat (Young's Ridge)

Grande Jorasses, East Ridge (descent)

Brouillard Ridge of Mont Blanc

Grand Jorasses, West Ridge

Grepon, Merde Glace Face

Gspaltenhorn, RotZahn Ridge

Young also soloed the Grand Cornier and led the first ascent of the Nesthron North East Ridge. He had amazing strength, evident from the fact that in one day he climbed the tops of Mont Rosa, Lyskamm, Castor and back to Lyskamm. Another difficult one day climb saw him top out on Charmoz, Grepon and Blaitiere.

During the First World War Young served with the British Ambulance Corps and lost his left leg in action. Upon his return to England Young designed, and with the help of a friend in a back yard workshop, manufactured an artificial leg that would allow him to climb. He made many climbs in the Alps including the Matterhorn. Young's last ascent occurred in 1935 on the Zinal Rothorn.

Young was responsible for founding the British Mountaineering Council.

By profession Young was an educator. He was himself educated at Marlborough and at Trinity College, Cambridge. At Trinity he was awarded the Chancellor's medal for English verse. He studied at Jena and Geneva, after which he became assistant master at Eton. He later became inspector of secondary schools, consultant to the Rockefeller Foundation in Europe and reader in comparative education at Cordon University.

As a poet Young also achieved some distinction. He published several volumes of poetry: **Wind and Hill, Freedom**, and **April and Rain**. In prose he wrote three outstanding mountain books: **Mountain Craft, On High Hills, and Mountains With a Difference**, as well as many articles for the *Alpine Journal*.

He was awarded an Honorary Doctorate of letters from Durham University. He was Alpine Club vice president in 1938 and in 1941 became president and served as such until 1944. He was also a fellow of the Royal Geographical Society.

He married Eleanor Slingsby and had one son.

Escape From Convention:

Geoffrey Winthrop Young

On May 2, 1956, G. W. Young was invited to deliver the seventeenth W. P. Ker Memorial Lecture at the University of Glasgow. It is not surprising that he chose to center his remarks on mountains. The title of his address: "The Influence of Mountains Upon the Development of Human Intelligence." This essay may well be one of the most important and least read examinations of mountains and their influence on art and intellect ever written. It comes not as a direct result of a particular climb, but as the result of a life spent in the mountains actively pursuing their physical and spiritual rewards. This, coupled with his outstanding scholarly pursuits, enables G. W. Young to understand more fully than most, what mountains and mountaineering contribute to the physical and spiritual evolution of man.

"The Influence of Mountains Upon the Deveolpent of Human Inteligence" traces the historical and intellectual development of human consciousness and the part mountains as abstract and concrete objects have played in it. Denoted clearly are the early human superstitions attached to the mountain brought on by human's innate fear of the unknown; and yet, as humans progressed and gained knowledge of the valleys, the mystery of the mountains they drew closer and closer to them. An excellent example of this phenomenon is found in the experiences of the early Puritan settlers in America. It was never the intention of the Puritan leaders to explore the wilderness for its own sake; the purpose was to subdue the wilderness and place it under the control of humans. It was believed that in the wild forests lurked evil and that humans would be swallowed up by it if they did not subdue it. This idea is much the same as that of the inhabitants of the valleys below the great European mountains, who felt that on the summits were monsters, dragons, or possibly even gods; but the summits were places not meant for humans.

The destructive elements the Puritans believed existed in wilderness is similar to what Woodrow Wilson Sayre analyzed in his essay "Why Men Do Climb." He said that too much "aloneness" is not good for human as they are social animals. Young recognizes that modern humans have what he calls an "awakened appreciation" for the mountains which is the result of individual courage shown by those who dared violate the mysterious realm of mountains and then had the continued drive to chronicle their experiences.

This record of mountain beauty is largely the product of early poets and philosophers such as John Ruskin who followed the romantic traditions set by Rouseau which, as Young states allowed, the "later nineteenth century to escape from this convention" meaning the myth of mountains and wild places as evil. The early supporters of mountain beauty largely wandered in the valleys around mountains but were cognizant of the size of mountains as well as their rugged beauty, and thus used the inspiration derived from them as part of their imagination expressed in art, music, poetry, paintings, etc. The poets and seers naturally led others after them and so the natural evolution was from valley to ridge and from ridge to face for the mountain rambler. This evolution then produced a literature of its own: Mountain Literature.

Young states that the canon of mountain literature lacks the substance for it to generate scholarly interest because of its thinness—its lack of depth. This may well be true of the early journal accounts of climbs, but maybe his being so close to it he is blinded by its brilliance—like Coleridge, Young may be his own harshest critic. If the scholarly world were to rely on the few poems by Shelley, Byron, Wordsworth and Ruskin that mention mountains it would indeed be thin. The essays generated by the actual climbers, who from the beginning were serious about alpine exploration and were the most educated and financially able members of society, who were looking for justification for such risky recreation and did so by listing the intrinsic benefits of climbing such as the physical, psychological and spiritual rewards of the individual. They also created a microcosm which could be carefully examined by the reader of the mountain essays who could then apply or reject the observation of the actual climber in their own life. It is this kind of depth that makes mountaineering essays of substantial literary substance.

According to Young mountain literature gained literary respectability when men like Leslie Stephen and John Tyndall picked up alpen-stock and pen as well. As mentioned earlier, Rousseau and Ruskin enabled Stephen and others to break the conventions that limited mountaineering literature. This recognition by the scholarly world was of the utmost importance:

> This recognition, or awareness, of an innate mountain feeling almost amounted to a secondary "breakthrough" in our evolutionary progress. Its revelation has led to the deliberate pursuit of mountain exploration over all the globe, and to a hurried flood of record. In this we might have found the answer to our question as to the origin of our feeling. But here an invariable human change, one belonging to the history of all our arts, again impedes us: the steady shift of emphasis from inspiration to skill, from impression or inspiration to personal performance. Record; in the beginning concerned only with the discovery of novel beauty, with the mountains themselves and the human response to them, has tended always more, and more rapidly, to concentrate upon the human achievement. We must look elsewhere than in conscious recording. Of greater interest to us than any mountaineering stories of our modern response, emotional or, judgmatic, to natural scenery must be a consideration of the remoter ages during which that judgment was being formed and that aesthetic sense developed, and of the conditions, climatic or scenic, which inspired and guided those beginnings. (Young 94)

This acceptance placed restraints on the writers of essays. No longer could verbose description pass itself off as legitimate; the writing needed to be deeper—it needed to explore not only the actual beauty of mountains as the physical joys of the ascent but had to examine the deeper reasons for human desire to climb. This meant that mountain essay needed to deal with things in the context of history and provide the developmental reasons for human willingness to leave the security of their "cave" to ascend the unknown heights for only intrinsic rewards.

The essay must defend the concept of "ascent for its own sake." The way this was done by Stephen, Tyndall, Mummery and others was to explore the psychological implications which lead to moral questions like "How can humans justify risking life for internal reward alone?"

This requirement presented an enormous problem for the mountaineer\writer. It is difficult to convince even those who live in the hills like the man with the ox-cart in Frost's poem "The Mountain" that climbing is worthwhile:

It doesn't seem so much to climb a mountain you've worked around the foot of all your life. What would I do? Go in my overalls, with a big stick, the same as when the cows haven't come down to the bars at milking time? Or with a shotgun for a stray black bear? 'Twouldn't seem real to climb for climbing it. (Lathem 40-44)

From this perspective—that cliff should be viewed from afar—the job of the mountaineer/writer is that of cultural conditioning or actually cultural re-conditioning—to break down age-old psychological barriers when they create blindness or necessary tolerance for dangerous things like mountains. Mountains are taken for granted sometimes by those who live in them, or at least close to them, which results in a failure to see not only their beauty but their necessity as a source of aesthetic and physical challenge.

The result can be what Young states has happened in the past:

During the long evolution of man there have been, of course, forerunners partially anticipating an aesthetic awareness; artists among the cave men, who decorated the rocks with an abstract vision of animal life. There have been also northerners who became poets as they wandered alone year after year on fell and moorland; Scottish crofters and Kerry cottagers whose solitude among mountains made of them Greek and Latin scholars, religious visionaries, or romantic ballad-mongers and story-tellers. But it was not specifically their mountains that made them so; nor did they become lovers of mountains in our sense. It was the long communion in solitude with their home world, with natural surroundings so familiar as to frame but never to interrupt thought, which produced them. All solitary living with nature can effect this, even to the production of a supreme ploughman poet upon open plains. In the evolution of human intelligence these more sensitized or dynamic beings have been the necessary precursors, assuring progress in culture. In certain instances the sympathy with nature has been so intense that they have experienced a sense of mystical fusion with the natural world about them. (Young 96-97)

The mountain becomes a symbol, one that contradicts the "level habits of earth." It becomes a place for learning the great mysteries of life. There is some history here in that mountains have always, at least to the poet, been a place to seek enlightenment. One only need look at the Bible to find the history of inspiration found in high places. A mountain in the story of Noah became the re-starting place for the human race after the flood (**Genesis** 8:4). For Moses it was a place of instruction and revelation where he received from God the ten commandments; the touchstone of Judaic and Christian religious philosophy (**Exodus** chapters 19 and 20). For Isaiah the mountains represented a place of peace and security: "The mountain of the Lord's house shall be established in the tops of the mountains. . . let us go up to the mountain of the Lord . . . and he will teach us of his ways, and we will walk in his paths" (**Isaiah** 2:2-5). Christ received testing and instruction in the mountains (**Matthew** 4:8) as well as using them himself as a place to teach his followers (**Matthew** chapters 5-7).

Young's essay is making a point that differs from that of other mountain writers. Mountains, particularly the way in which they surround Athens, have imperceptibly formed human consciousness, leading to the perfect balance between reason and feeling that made Greece the source of Western thought, and that perspective has influenced humanity ever since.

History illustrates the special place mountains have held in the past. Is it any surprise that humans naturally look to mountains as sources of inspiration? Mountains represent a place of renewal, of rebirth which draw humans toward them. This desire to visit and climb the mountains will always be alive in humanity regardless of the efforts of technology to make humans soft; their mind, their memory will pull them toward the pearls. Human potential is unlimited and climbing recognizes it:

However mechanised, or automatised, the conditions of human life may become, the same number of human beings will, I believe, continue to carry this inherited memory, reinforced for action by the new awareness of mountains and of mountaineering which has come with this last century. There will be men and women who find among hills forgetfulness of fear and of their anxieties, in the restoration of their sense of proportion, the recovery, of reasonable measure, which was the mountains' original gift to men; or who, like Smuts and like so many, will see again upon the mountains spirits of religion—true symbols, founded upon the same inspiring mountain principles of measure, proportion, order, and of an uprightness which points a way beyond clouds and, at least, towards the stars. (Young 115-116)

Geoffrey Winthrop Young

SIR JOHN HUNT

*O*f the authors in this study Sir John Hunt is certainly the most diverse in activities. He has participated in exploration, war, social and educational reform. Yet each of his activities has had one common denominator—that of leadership.

John Hunt was educated at Marlborough College and The Royal Military College at Sandhurst. Commissioned in 1930, his attachments were to Kings Royal Rifle Corps, which he later commanded, Indian Police, Indian Infantry Brigade, Middle Eastland Corps, and Western Europe Commander's-in-Chief Committee. Promoted to the rank of colonel, Hunt was assigned to General Staff Headquarters (British) Corps and in 1953 became the Assistant Commandant at The Staff College. Upon his retirement from military service in 1956, he was awarded Honorary Brigadier.

After his military retirement Hunt became director of the Duke of Edinburgh's Award Scheme and Rector of Aberdeen University from 1968 to 1970. Hunt served as a personal adviser to the Prime Minister during the Nigerian Civil War. He has also served on several advisory committees dealing with police and probation officers.

The achievements in Hunt's life that qualify him for this study are his achievements in mountaineering. As a young man Hunt learned his mountain craft in the Alps where he completed numerous routes. He was a pioneer Alpine climber in the Himalayas and Karakoram and participated in joint expeditions with Russian climbers in both the Caucasus and Pamirs. Hunt has also explored the unclimbed parts of the Yukon and Greenland.

The most important achievement in climbing for Hunt occurred in the summer of 1953 when, as leader of the British Mount Everest expedition, he saw Edmund Hilary and Tenzing Norkay stand atop the earth's highest pinnacle, the 29,002 foot summit of Mount Everest.

Sir John Hunt was president of the Alpine Club from 1956-1958, of the Climber's Club from 1963-1966, of the British Mountaineering Council from 1965-1968. He was an Honorary fellow of the Royal Geographical Society and its president in 1977.

His awards, like his activities are many: Order 1st Class Gurka Right Hand, Indian Everest Medal, Hubbard Medal (United States), Founder's Medal-Royal Geographical Society, Lawrence Memorial Medal. He was knighted in 1953 and created life peer in 1966.

Hunt was the author of three books in the mountaineering genre: *The Conquest of Everest, Our Everest Adventure* and *Red Snows.*

The Quest Metaphor:

Sir John Hunt

Sir John Hunt epitomizes the British citizen, well schooled, tireless servant of the crown, honorable and undaunted in physical and mental achievement. Hunt's leadership of the successful 1953 Everest expedition serves as a personal as well as collective victory for Hunt and England.

That Hunt should be on an Everest expedition let alone lead the successful one rings of poetic justice. In 1936 the British medical board judged him not fit enough for the rigors of the 1936 Everest Expedition—which failed.

John Hunt's contributions to the literature are in three books mentioned in the biography preceding this section, but the work selected for this study is his essay "Reflections" which appears as chapter eighteen in *The Conquest of Everest*. This particular essay was chosen for several reasons 1) Hunt clearly addresses the innate impulse in man to explore. The term modern psychology has attached to this clearly recognizable trait is "The Ulysses Factor." 2) It also reflects Bonnatti's concern of man becoming spiritually dead for lack of adventure and physical achievements. 3) Hunt recognizes the problems postulated by William James in his essay "The Moral Equivalent of War" and provides what appears to be a useful answer to what James saw as a serious human dilemma. 4) This essay, whether Hunt intended it as such or not, works as an allegory for the social development of humans. Hunt, after seeing his dream realized, continues to look to the future of mountaineering with the eye of the prophet as he sees the possibility for even greater physical, spiritual and psychological achievements to come after the Conquest of Everest.

Hunt pays tribute to the "other expeditions" for their developmental contribution to his expedition's success, for as with the growth and development of human life, each generation being greatly indebted to the previous one for testing and keeping those traits necessary for progress and the systematic elimination of those traits that are useless, so also was Hunt to those expedition leaders who preceded him. This entire concept can be applied both scientifically and socially, since scientific thought as well as social development is entirely indebted to those who laid the foundations for those next in line to build upon. As Mary Shelley's Professor Waldman states in his conversation with Victor Frankenstein, speaking of the Alchemists Cornelius Agrippa and Paracelsus:

These were men to whose indefatigable zeal modern philosophers were indebted for most of the foundations of their knowledge....
The labors of men of genius, however erroneously directed, scarcely ever fail in ultimately turning to the solid advantage of mankind. (Shelley, **Frankenstein** 41)

Hunt approaches recognition of his predecessors with the same sort of heartfelt gratitude:

The significance of all these other attempts is that, regardless of the height they reached, each one added to the mounting sum of experience, and this experience had to reach a certain total before the riddle could be solved. The building of this pyramid of experience was vital to the whole issue; only when it had attained a certain height was it within the power of any team of mountaineers to fashion its apex. Seen in this light, other expeditions did not fail; they made progress. They had reached this stage when we prepared to try again last winter. By that time, but not before, the defenses by which the mountain had so far withstood assault were well enough known; it only remained to study them and draw the right conclusions in order to launch yet one more party which would have every weapon—material and human—with which to do battle against Everest. We of the 1953 Everest Expedition are proud to share the glory with our predecessors. (Hunt 127)

To add to his praise of his forerunners he attaches mythical significance to their feats which he refers to as the "Quest." The Quest metaphor creates a vision of the brave exploits of Jason, Aeneas and Ulysses.

A term applied to those who search for adventure, willingly facing danger, is the "Ulysses Factor." J.R.L. Anderson in his book *The Ulysses Factor*, subtitled "The Exploring Instinct in Man," traces the exploring instinct through several stages. The anthropological stage follows quite closely the evolutionary process of adaption:

> The anthropological approach remains: There is some factor in man, some form of special adaption, which prompts a few individuals to exploits which, however purposeless they may seem, are of value to the survival of the race (17).

> The Ulysses factor appears to be unique to man. Other animals have a sense of adventure and certainly enjoy hunting, but deliberate risk-taking in pursuit of a goal of no apparent practical value is not the habit of any other animal other than man.(Anderson 20)

Hunt sums up this same theory in similar terms. He praises the earlier climbers for their example, persistence and determination: "for this compelling urge to continue the struggle, we have above all else to thank the earlier Everest climbers" (Hunt *128)*.

Anderson and other researchers maintain that with earlier man, war and hunting satisfied the urge to explore, but as William James states in "The Moral Equivalent For War" modern man rejects the adventure of war and that in itself creates a serious problem, because as Anderson explains, there is something in adventure that is essential to human very existence—even survival. These ideas are metaphoric, adventure is like war in certain respects, in that it calls on those virtues which Anderson lists in the latter part of his passage:

> All these beliefs of mine put me squarely into the anti-militarist party. But I do not believe that peace either ought to be or will be permanent on this globe, unless the states specifically organized preserve some of the old elements of army-discipline. A permanently successful peace-economy cannot be a simple pleasure-economy. In the more or less socialistic future towards which mankind seems drifting we must still subject ourselves collectively to

those severities which answer to our real position upon this only partly hospitable globe. We must make new energies and hardihoods continue the manliness to which the military mind so faithfully clings. Martial virtues must be the enduring cement; intrepidity, contempt of softness, surrender of private interest, obedience to command, must still remain the rock upon which states are built—unless, indeed, we wish for dangerous reactions against commonwealths fit only for contempt, and liable to invite attack whenever a centre of crystallization for military-minded enterprise gets formed anywhere in their neighborhood. (Anderson 323)

Hunt sees the activity of the expedition, a military exercise of sort which provides the cement needed to help humans and society together. The climbing expedition must be orderly, as should society, and should invite unity in order for it to succeed.

Next in the order of events I would place sound, thorough, meticulously detailed planning. On Everest, the problems of organization assume the proportions of a military campaign; I make no apology for this comparison, or for the fact that we planned the ascent of Everest on these lines. It was thanks to this that we were able not only to foresee our needs in every detail—guided by previous experience provided by others, we judged aright—but to have constantly before us a clear program to carry out at every stage: the march-out; acclimatization; preparation of the Icefall, the first and second stages of the build-up; reconnaissance and preparation of the Lhotse Face; even, in outline, the assault plan itself. These were the aims to be achieved by given dates, and achieve each and all of them we would, and did....

Above all else, I should like to stress our unity as a party. This was undoubtedly the biggest single factor in the final result, for the ascent of Everest, perhaps more than most human ventures, demanded a very high degree of selfless co-operation; no amount of equipment or food could have compensated for any weakness in this respect. (Hunt 128, 131)

This cement not only binds society but prevents the stagnation of humanity, Bonnatti's fear of overcivilization. Such achievement is valuable not only to those individuals who actually participate, but to the society they represent. "Was it worth while" Hunt asks? Which is a question that must be answered by all, participant and observer alike. Was it beneficial only to those who actually were there? What benefit does it provide the whole human family? It appears from Hunt's essay that even though relatively few were actually involved, the whole expedition was an ensign to the rest of humankind because it provides an example of societal unity on a small scale, one that could possibly be developed on a much larger scale. In mountaineering this has been attempted with great success. Political barriers, language and cultural barriers have been transcended in the form of multi-nation expeditions, each new one building on both the successes and failures of those before.

Was it worth while? For us who took part in the venture was so beyond doubt. We have shared a high endeavor; we have witnessed scenes of beauty and grandeur; we have built up a lasting comradeship among ourselves and we have seen the fruits of that comradeship ripen into achievement. We shall not forget those moments of great living upon that mountain.

The story of the ascent of Everest is one of teamwork. If there is a deeper and more lasting message behind our venture than the mere ephemeral sensation of a physical feat, I believe this to be the value of comradeship and the many virtues which combine to create it. Comradeship, regardless of race or creed, is forged among high mountains, through the difficulties and dangers to which they expose those who aspire to climb them, the need to combine their efforts to attain their goal, the thrills of a great adventure shared together. (Hunt 134)

The essays of men like Hunt are the means by which the message and experience of the climber is passed on.

Ultimately, the justification for climbing Everest, if any justification is needed, will lie in the seeking of their "Everests" by others, stimulated by this event as we were inspired by others before us. From the response to the news of our success, not only in our own country and Commonwealth but also in many other lands, it seems clear that the zest for adventure is still alive everywhere. Before, during, and especially after the expedition, we received countless gifts and messages of good will and delight, in both prose and verse, from all over the world, from heads of governments and humble folk alike. Very many of these messages were sent by children and young people. The ascent of Everest seems to have stirred the spirit of adventure latent in every human breast. (Hunt 135)

The ascent of Everest is one of humanity's great adventures and it illustrates human potential for other great adventures, each of which leads to the expansion of the spirit which overshadows any other form of compensation and, in fact, justifies humans as explorers.

With Hunt's expedition results of extrinsic value also came from the ascent of Everest: a special school to educate the sherpa boys regarding the "love and craft" of mountaineering. Sir Edmund Hillary has for the past 40 years devoted his life, and his family has willingly followed, in providing education in all forms to the people of the Himalayas.

Hunt's vision of the continued evolution of climbing is clear with his mention of the possibilities of ascents of high peaks without oxygen (the most important of all the 1953 expedition tools) as well as traverses and solo ascents, all of which have now been done but which in Hunt's day seemed impossible. Most important from a humanistic standpoint was Hunt's dream of all of Everest being opened—free from political barriers, to allow climbers to work on climbing problems without concern from politics. This too has happened as evidenced by the 1982 American ascent of Everest's north (Chinese) face.

Great literature is timeless, provides universal truths that transcend all human barriers-language, philosophy, politics, culture, race and religion. The universal truth which makes Hunt's essay important is the recognition of the infinite possibilities attainable by the spirit of humanity:

There are many other opportunities for adventure, whether they be sought among the hills, in the air, upon the sea, in the bowels of the earth, or on the ocean bed; and there is always the mood to reach. There is no height, no depth, that the spirit of man, guided by a higher spirit, cannot attain. (Hunt 137)

MAURICE HERZOG

*M*aurice Herzog, an Alpinist and French politician was born in Lyon in 1919, the son of Robert Herzog, an engineer, and Germaine Beaume. He studied law in Paris, returning to Lyon afterwards to pursue studies in science and business.

In 1964 he married Marie-Pierre de Cosse-Brissac, by whom he had two children, Laurent and Felicite. He subsequently married Elisabeth Gamper, who bore two more children, Sebastien and Mathias.

Herzog served as president of the Kleber-Colombes Corporation from 1945 to 1958 during which time he also led French expeditions to the Himalayas. The group, including L. Lacheual, Gaston Rebuffat, and Lionel Terray climbed Annapurna on June 3, 1950; it was the first time a peak over 8,000 meters had been climbed. Herzog and Lachenal both suffered severe frostbite of the hands and feet.

Herzog devoted much of his energy to politics in the following years. He served as Commissioner of Youth and Sports, and as Secretary General of the National Committee on Sports. He was elected to public office as a representative from the Rhone district, while continuing his involvement with youth sports programs at the national level. In 1963 he was elevated to Secretary of State for Youth and Sports where he served until 1966. He then spent several years as a consultant in economic, social, scientific and cultural areas. In 1967 he was again elected to public office, serving from 1967-1978 as a representative from the Haut-Savoie. He received important committee and elective assignments while in government, and reported on developments in space exploration and atomic research. He was the founder and president of a government group concerned with science and technology. He was mayor of Chamonix from 1968 to 1977. In 1970 he accepted an appointment to the International Olympic Committee. Since the mid 1960's he has held numerous managerial positions in French corporations, and has accepted special parliamentary assignments in scientific and nuclear affairs. In 1981 he was made president of the Mont-Blanc Tunnel Society.

His publications include: *Annapurna Premier 8000* (Annapurna: The First 8000 Meter Climb), *Regards sur l'Annapurna* (A Look at Annapurna), *L' Expedition de l' Annapurna* (The Annapurna Expedition), *La Montagne* (The Mountain) *Les Grandes Aventures de l' Himalaya* (The Great Adventures of the Himalayas).

He has been awarded the Legion of Honor medal, the War Cross 39-45, and the Commander of Sports Merit. He still enjoys golf and some climbing and is honorary president of the French Alpine Club.

The Ultimate Bond:

Maurice Herzog

*W*hile in the American hospital at Neailly, Maurice Herzog dictated an essay that among mountain literature is perhaps, the most physically graphic, dealing closely with actual suffering. But Herzog's explanation transcends the bounds of physical suffering and conveys a spiritual meaning to the reader about why humans climb mountains.

Unlike most mountain literature, Herzog's account is written in a narrative form and is colloquial in style. The account is based mostly on Herzog's memory but is sustained by information taken from the official expedition log, which was kept by Marcel Ichac, and also by Louis Lachenal's private journal. Where other writers have felt it important to dwell on the spiritual rewards of the climb and have chosen to overlook, or at least not emphasize the physical struggles, Herzog has used the physical to convey the divine nature of human; their ability to adapt to the most difficult of situations, and more importantly man's ability to survive physically and grow spiritually. The concept of community action is apparent in the works of the writers examined in this collection and is clearly illustrated in Herzog's as well. It is safe to say that the expedition represents human need for companionship with their own kind. In Herzog's essay the concept of community is illustrated in the graphic terms of a make-shift surgery in a tent at 20,000 feet on the flanks of Annapurna. It picks up after Herzog and Lachenal had reached the summit and had returned snow-blind and frost bitten to Camp II. Herzog's record of his sufferings as the cost for Annapurna's summit can only make the reader ask "Why?" then read on in search of the answer.

It has been noted in the works of most mountain writers that to be joined by the rope is the ultimate bond of friendship. In the case of Herzog and his companions this bond is further strengthened by the events that occur after the rope is untied—in the surgery and on the path back to France.

> Night fell gradually. Oudot made his preparations, requisitioned Ichac and Schatz as nurses, and Camp II was turned into a hospital. In cold and discomfort, and to the accompaniment of continual avalanches, these men fought late in the night to save their friends. Armed with torches they passed from tent to tent, bending over the wounded and giving them emergency treatment, at this minute camp, perched 20,000 feet up on the flanks of one of the highest mountains in the world. (Herzog 149-150)

The painful work of Dr. Oudot and the pain for Ichac and Schatz, who helped with the excruciating injections used to stimulate circulation in the severely frost-bitten hands and feet of Herzog, Lachenal, Terray and Rebuffat, as well as the personal recognition by Herzog of the forthcoming loss of his fingers and toes illustrate clearly the fortitude of man. Such heroism has been the theme of much of literature beginning with the earliest stories of humankind's quest. It is found in the *Odyssey, Beowulf, Morte d'Arthur* and is apparent in the literature of all ages.

Along with the great personal strength shown by heroes like Herzog, the one thing that makes his courage representative of all humans is his admission to weakness. This recognition is partly due to a semi-isolated state—his blindness. The concept of too much isolation as having serious psychological effects is illustrated by Conrad in *Heart of Darkness*, and Mary Shelley in *Frankenstein*. These are fictional, of course, yet Herzog's feelings are supported in actual accounts by survivors as to the horrible effects of too much "aloneness." This can be seen in Peter Freuchen's *Arctic Adventures* and George Stewart's account of the Donner Party in *Ordeal by Hunger*, where even though they were in a group the isolation was so great that those surviving set aside the proprieties of civilization, and like the fictional Mr. Kurtz, collectively lapsed into cannibalism.

Herzog's semi-isolated personal state, coupled with the actual physical isolation of being at 20,000 feet on the mountain, brings about a longing for the security and safety found in the familiar, and forces him to find strength within himself to endure his sufferings:

The performance was repeated on the other leg. My nerves were all to pieces, and to brace myself like this took all of my strength. In went the needle and I howled and sobbed miserably, but tried in vain to keep still. I could see nothing because of the bandage. If only I could have seen the faces of my friends it might perhpas have helped me. But I was in the dark—a terrible darkness—with nowhere to look for consolation but within myself. It was late and we had all had more than enough. Then for that day it was over and the first-aid party moved on to Lachenal's tent. He perhaps, would have more courage in face of physical pain. (Herzog 152)

The accounts of man's risky adventures serve several important purposes. Knowing what those who have ventured out before have encountered one is able, even to the saving of oneself, to avoid certain dangers. In the case of Herzog's group this perspective is illustrated by Ichac's knowledge of the British Nanda Devi expedition led by Tilman which was held up for weeks by swollen rivers due to the monsoon which was fast approaching for the Annapurna group. This knowledge was possibly the reason Herzog and the other injured survived because it forced the expedition to move even when the injuries would have dictated otherwise.

This historical knowledge carries over to more personal and relative areas, including Herzog's recognition of Oudot's position as expedition doctor and the grim responsibilities connected with it. Herzog, unlike many, was grateful for Oudot's courage rather than developing a hatred for him by thinking his actions directed at Herzog personally and thus blaming Oudot for the loss of his fingers and toes. The recognition that his suffering is not unique is also a strong plus for Herzog—but this recognition came because of his knowledge of the past:

I appreciated Oudot's courage and was grateful to him for not being afraid to tell me the extent of the amputations which he foresaw would be necessary. He treated me as a man and as a friend, with courage and frankness, which I shall never forget.

The injections, which had already done so much good, had to be repeated. This time the session would be even worse and I was terrified at the prospect. I am ashamed to say that the thought of this treatment daunted me, and yet so many people have had to endure it. (Herzog 154)

The uniqueness of a human being as compared to other animals is their ability to reason. The ability to reason is paramount as to why humans sit at the current pinnacle of the evolutionary process because reason allows them to adapt and survive. Many times the adaptability and survivability is due to their innate social instincts which allow humans to make group decisions and then carry those decisions out in harmony. Herzog illustrates this concept clearly with his discussion of the evacuation process involving two different cultures working in harmony. The language barriers as well as the cultural barriers are transcended with devotion to the common cause—a reverance for life and individual importance to the group. This individual and collective importance is clearly the theme of John Donne's "Devotions":

> All mankinde is of one Author, and is one volume; when one Man dies, one Chapter is not torne out of the book, but translated into a better language; and every chapter must be translated; God imploies several translators; some peeces are translated by age, some by sicknesse, some by warre, some by justice; but God's hand is in every translation; and his hand shall binde up all our scattered leaves againe, for that Librarie where every booke shall lie open to one another.

> No man is an Iland intire of itselfe; every man is a peece of the Continent, a part of the maine; if a clod bee washed away by the Sea, Europe is the lesse, as well as if a promontorie were, as well as if a manor of thy friends or of thine owne were; any man's death diminishes me, because I am involved in Mankinde; and therefore never send to know for whom the bell tolls; it tolls for thee. (Donne 528)

Likewise Herzog calls to mind this same idea of the collective importance of individuals with his commentary on his evacuation.

In a situation like the evacuation process one who formerly was the motivation behind the initial activity suddenly becomes the need for the activity—the burden, and cannot participate in the effort despite the possible demoralizing effect. This case is especially true in the context of an expedition where the very survival of the group depends on the full participation of each member. If one lets down, the problems are obvious. The concept is the same as in early societies where each member was relied upon for the survival of the whole as in **Proverbs** 6:3 "Go to the ant, thou sluggard; consider her ways, and be wise." Ants are noted for their communal ethics—each member works and produces for the good of the group. It is easy to see and feel Herzog's frustration at becoming the burden.

> Ichac briefly explained what was going on. Being blind was most demoralizing; I felt I was nothing but a chattel to be carted about. I knew my opthalmia was less serious than that of the others and I kept asking for the bandage to be taken off. But since I was nothing but a chattel I had no right to speak. (Herzog 163)

Yet one who views this scenario from afar can see that he, of all those involved, should feel no regrets.

Herzog's emphasis of his physical loss is the only way he could communicate to his readers the price he was willing to pay for the intrinsic rewards the climb provided:

> I think that the fingers of your left hand will have to be amputated, but I hope to be able to save the end joints of your right hand fingers. If all goes well, you'll have passable hands. As for your feet, I'm afraid that all your toes will have to go, but that won't prevent you from walking. Of course to begin with it'll be difficult, but you'll adapt yourself all right, you'll see. (Herzog 165-166)

Herzog discusses his realization of the ultimate results the amputations will bring. He meets it with the same tenacity and conviction that led him to the summit of Annapurna. His friend, Terray rewards this heroic display with love and comfort:

> "Oh but Lionel, everything's over for me, and I simply can't bear what they're doing to me any longer."
>
> "Life's not over," he insisted, "you'll see France again, and Chamonix."
>
> It was out at last, I had told him, and I let myself go in despair:
>
> "I'll never be able to climb again—I'll never do the Eiger now, Lionel, and I wanted to so much."

Sobs choked me. My head was against Terray's and I felt his tears, for he was crying, too. He was the only one who could fully understand the tragedy that this represented for me, and I could see that to him, too, it appeared hopeless.

"No, of course, not the Eiger, but I'm sure you'll be able to go back to the mountains. . ." and then, very hesitantly, he added, "Not the same sort of climbs as before, of course."

"It will never be the same again. But, Lionel, even if I can't do the sort of climbs I used to, if I could still do easy things, that would be a great deal. The mountains meant everything to me—I spent the best days of my life among them—I don't want to do spectacular climbs, or famous ones, but I want to be able to enjoy myself in the mountains, even if it's only on the old standard routes."

"You'll go back all right, you'll see," said Lionel. "I feel just the same way."

"But mountains aren't the only thing; there are other things in life as well—what shall I do about all that?"

"You'll manage somehow, Maurice."

There was a silence; then he said, "You ought to lie down now."

He settled me with such affectionate care that he accomplished the impossible and left me comforted and soothed. After a last look to see that I was comfortable, he went slowly out. What a friend I had found in Terray! (Herzog 168-169)

The farther away from the mountains Herzog gets and the closer he gets to the technical world the more he appreciates the amenities and comforts that technology provides, probably because they represent safety "there was furniture—a table—a refrigerator!" Yet the scars of isolation—the deadened sensibilities—became more and more real. The mountains that had represented escape now became something to escape from:

The others were far ahead. The jolting began again, bearing me away from what would soon be nothing but memories. In the gentle languor into which I let myself sink, I tried to evisage my first contact with the civilized world in the homeward-bound airplane, and the terrible shock of landing at Orly and meeting family and friends.

But I could never have imagined the violent emotional shock that I should in fact experience when it came to the point, nor the sudden nervous depression which would then take hold of me. Those surgical operations in the field, the sickening butchery that shook even the toughest of the natives had gradually deadened our sensibilities; we were no longer able to judge the horror of it all. A toe snapping off and thrown away, useless, blood flowing and spurting, the unbearable smell from suppurating wounds—all this left us unmoved.

In the airplane before landing, Lachenal and I would be putting on fresh bandages for our arrival. But the minute we started down that iron ladder, all those friendly eyes looking at us with such pity, would at once tear aside the masks behind which we had sheltered. We were not to be pitied—and yet, the tears in those eyes and the expressions of distress, would suddenly bring me face to face with reality. A strange consolation for my sufferings to have brought me!

Rocked in my stretcher, I meditated on our adventure now drawing to a close, and on our unexpected victory. One always talks of the ideal as a goal towards which one strives but which one never reaches. For every one of us, Annapurna was an ideal that had been realized. In our youth we had not been misled by fantasies, nor by the bloody battles of modern warfare which feed the imagination of the young. For us the mountains had been a natural field of activity where, playing on the frontiers of life and death, we had found the freedom for which we were blindly groping and which was as necessary to us as bread. The mountains had bestowed on us their beauties, and we adored them with a child's simplicity and revered them with a monk's veneration of the divine.

Annapurna, to which we had gone emptyhanded, was a treasure on which we should live the rest of our days. With this realization we turn the page: a new life begins.

There are other Annapurnas in the lives of men. (Herzog 187-189)

Even with the terrible physical loss and suffering experienced by Herzog and his comrades, it is still clear that all they had endured was worth the cost. They attained an ideal and the reward was spiritually intrinsic, the very thing that justifies climbing as a worthwhile activity.

Woodrow Wilson Sayre

*W*oodrow Wilson Sayre occupies an unusual place in the history of mountaineering in that he is a twentieth century mountaineer with the hardihood and romantic vision of a "Golden Age" adventurer. He and his small band of fellow adventurers attempted, in 1962, what is only today being considered as possible and then only with the most up-to-date, state of the art equipment; a 25 mile traverse of the Himalayas at an average altitude of 20,000 ft. carrying all their own supplies and without any support team in an attempt to climb Everest's north wall. Though unsuccessful in the sense of reaching the summit, Sayre and his three companions did inspire a new generation of Himalayan climbers as well as presenting a new expedition philosophy—that of going light and without the aid of oxygen. In the words of Eric Shipton, the great British Himalayan climber: "To have got so far as you did by that long and arduous route and with the slender resources at your disposal was a magnificent achievement."

He is the grandson of American President Woodrow Wilson. His father was Ambassador Frances B. Sayre. He was educated at Williams College and received both his M.A. and Ph.D. from Harvard University. During World War II he served as an officer in the Army Air Corps.

Aside from his Everest attempt he has climbed Mount McKinley and a number of lesser peaks in Europe and America.

Gary Hemming and John Harlin. L'Aguille du Fou, Face Sud '63

Woodrow Wilson Sayre

THE PARADOX OF ALONENESS:

WOODROW WILSON SAYRE

*T*his essay deals with what Woodrow Wilson Sayre calls the "intervals" of climbing, something he feels is neglected in the literature of mountaineering and reflects his romantic vision of the grand capabilities of humans.

Sayre tackles what has been the most-asked question dealing with mountaineering since de Saussure offered a prize for the first ascent of Mont Blanc in 1760. The problem with this question is that material reward as well as scientific reward has been ruled out. Men are driven by other reasons. J.R.L. Anderson in his work *The Ulysses Factor* argues it is a natural human instinct to explore—to seek adventure. Dr. Sol Ray Rosenthal states man's willingness to risk life in pursuit of mountain peaks is validated because of the "sense of heightened awareness" which results from dangerous physical activity. In his article in **Outside**, January 1981 Rob Schultheis maintains that:

> Risk taking is a sacred thing. Man's purest, oldest, most primitive religions are built around it: the lonely vision-fasting of the Plains Indians, the Walkabout of the Australian aborigines, the ritual mountain climbing of Tibetan Lamas and Nepalese shamans. Even today climbers run into tribal mystics high on peaks like Mount Kenya and Ama Dablam. Jamaican holy men of the Rastafarian cult still swim out to sea until they are completely exhausted; they then turn and try to make it back to shore alive. For them, it is a religious ceremony, a sort of meditation, to go deliberately to

one's limit and then push on beyond. You either get power or you die. (33)

Sayre recognized all of these reasons as well as some others. In analyzing the basic question as to why men climb and all its possible answers he determines it is not a question of motivation but of values:

Eventually, I realized the root of the difference. The question about climbing is not a question about motivation at all. If it were, then the answer, "I climb because I like to," would be a perfectly appropriate answer. It is really a question about relative values. What the question is really asking is: "Look, this mountain climbing business is dangerous. It costs money. It is hard, exhausting work. You have to disrupt the family to do it. Now what values do you gain from climbing mountains that can possibly offset these obvious *disvalues*?" (Sayre 203)

Sayre is a philosopher, one concerned specifically with values. He recognizes that these lie behind the usual questions and answers: he digs deeper.

First on my list, but not necessarily first in importance, I would mention beauty. There are the colors: black rock and ultramarine shadows, pure white swell of snow, turquoise and amethyst creavasses, and the diamond glitter of sun on ice. In the afterglow of sunset the air itself becomes pink and gold. And there are the infinite clean shapes: wind-carved snow, fluted ice, weathered stone, and cloud-brushed sky. Most of all, there are the great mountains themselves set in their rivers of ice, changing grandeur in every light and every weather. If a person will cross the ocean just to look at the beauty of a cathedral, why would he not do as much or more to see sights such as these? (Sayre 204)

This answer is similar to one that could come from a farmer as to why he farms in a time when he could make more money working in a factory, or from an early morning walk, or even a banker on a Tuesday afternoon at the golf course: because it is beautiful outside; it's nice to commune with nature.

Thoreau, in his essay "Walking," when he would go on his "expeditions" to the southwest of Concord along Marlborough Road, said he should do so intending adventure. In his theory Thoreau states that

" . . . In wildness is the preservation of the world . . . Life consists with wildness. The most alive is the wildness. Not yet subdued to man, its presence refreshed him" (242-243). Sayre too sees the same wild sanity when he visits the remote mountains:

> Very closely associated with the beauty of the mountains are some special emotions which the highest and wildest peaks provoke. I feel a special excitement when I look out over thousands of square miles of untouched country. I feel it again when I walk where only a handful of men have walked in the history of the world, when I explore some hidden ridge or crag, or when I make the first track across a great unbroken snow field. I feel a special happiness to be alone in the high, silent places of the world tucked close under the sky. Such things are worth a little insecurity and sacrifice. (Sayre 205)

The concept of "aloneness" as advocated by both Thoreau and Sayre is almost a Marcusian philosophical view in that society controls human life. Humans need to break away then from society, even if it is for a short time in order to free himself. A human in wildness is most free.

This view appears to conflict with John Hunt's concept that the expedition is a social microcosm of a successful society. Sayre recognizes this paradox. Because of his experience on Everest, with a small, lightweight expedition consisting of himself and only three others, as contrasted to Hunt's expedition with a cast of hundreds, Sayre can reconcile this seeming contradition. Whereas with Hunt's expedition they always climbed in pairs for any number of reasons—safety, economy, etc.—, Sayre's expedition, aside from being illegal (something of which Thoreau and Marcuse would probably have approved.) required many hours of solitary hiking as well as occasional teamwork.

> So this is a need which the mountains can fulfill. There are many hours, especially in a small expedition, when you walk the trails completely alone. And this aloneness depends in large part on unspoilt, untouched nature. I would say that there is need for alternation here to. We need to experience nature with the friendly marks upon it of human work and struggle and hope. But also we need to see nature apart from even the smallest sign of human interference. For this the high mountains are perfect. (Sayre 208)

This theory has had social application as in "high adventure therapy programs" used for delinquent youth. The theory behind such programs is to teach criminal youth that antisocial behavior is not the release they are seeking from a desensitized industrial world, but that release can be found in being a productive individual within social structures. This occurs in climbing. Each member of a climbing team must do the actual physical climb as an individual, as it is impossible to drag some non-contributor up the mountain as can be done in social settings. But it is possible that because of the tools and logistics of climbing the group can help the individual without removing his responsibilities, and the individual effort furthers the cause of the expedition, Sayre finds the real paradox in the fact that even though the model exists in the climbing environment, society itself doesn't seem to produce the "togetherness" in true companionship that it should:

> If it is a bit of a paradox that the mountains should provide both solitude and deep companionship, it is also a bit of a paradox that society should not provide those values. That is, in spite of all the crowded "togetherness" increasingly required of us, real companionship is nevertheless hard to find. And on the other hand, in spite of all the solitude—in the sense of loneliness—that there is in society today, nevertheless, the solitude that I have been describing is absent. It involves being alone where no voice reaches and no foot falls, where there can be and is no other sign of a human. Only then does the person turn deeply inward. Loneliness is not enough.

> Thus, mountain climbing tends to furnish an antidote to much that is wrong or overemphasized in society. The pendulum has swung much too far towards "togetherness"; mountaineering redresses the balance. Society tends to make human relationships superficial; mountaineering deepens them. Other values can be added. (Sayre 208-209)

Ironically, society causes the loss of friendship because of its fast-paced and superficial existence when in fact friendly relationships should be its end.

One thing upon which both Sayre and Hunt agree is human's militaristic nature and that climbing fulfills that requirement:

In most primitive societies this testing is an established custom. There is the hunting party, the war party, or games and rituals involving danger and difficulty. But in our society testing depends on individual initiative or on accident. In war, of course, men find the closeness of shared danger—the men of a gun crew or an infantry patrol, for example—but where else is the opportunity? At any rate mountain climbing is one way of providing it. (Sayre 206)

This is clearly a support of William James' "Moral Equivalent to War" theory:

Militarism is the great preserver of our ideals of hardihood, and human life with no use for hardihood would be contemptible. Without risks or prizes for the darer, history would be insipid indeed; and there is a type of military character which every one feels that the race should never cease to breed, for every one is sensitive to this superiority. The duty is incumbent on mankind, of keeping military characters in stock—of keeping them, if not for use, then as ends in themselves and as pure pieces of perfection,—so that Roosevelt's weaklings and mollycoddles may not end by making everything else disappear from the face of nature. (Sayre 316-317)

As much as mountaineers cheer solitude, Sayre takes a very realistic approach regarding it. In overtones and insights much like those of Joseph Conrad's in **Heart of Darkness and Lord Jim,** Sayre discusses the dangers of too much "aloneness." He recognized man as a social animal who, on occasion, needs to be totally isolated from his own kind much like the person in Frost's poem "A Lone Striker," who quits the factory, analogous to society, and retires to the wilderness:

He knew another place, a wood,

And in it, tall as trees, were cliffs;

• • •

He knew a path that wanted walking;

He knew a spring that wanted drinking;

A thought that wanted further thinking;

A love that wanted re-renewing.

Nor was this just a way of talking
To save him the expense of doing.
With him it boded action, deed.
He left but, he also left an opening to return:
If there should ever come a day
When industry seemed like to die
Because he left it in a lurch,
Come get him—they knew where to search. (Lathem 273-275)

Sayre states: "A man is unhappy unless he has both. He needs to be with his fellow man, and he needs to be apart form him" (Sayre 206-207).

Conrad's character, Mr. Kurtz, is a prime literary example of the effects of total moral isolation. He enters the jungle with noble intentions but eventually is consumed by passions that, being away from his fellows too long, run rampant: "But the wilderness had found him out early, and had taken on him a terrible vengeance" (133). The bounds of decency society places on man's animal impulses were totally removed by Kurtz's isolation and he became a savage who along with greed and lust for power, also became a cannibal, the ultimate form of immoral consumerism.

Jeff Long, in his short story entitled *"Cannibals,"* takes this Conradian doctrine and places it in a mountaineering context. The story places two climbers high on a Himalayan peak trapped by avalanches where they remain for days. The result of the "aloneness" is cannibalism—human consumerism. Such examples in fiction are supported in essays by those who have experienced such isolation, but to a lesser degree, such as Sayre.

Sayre's view of human "too much" is found in his "mold" metaphor which, like Loren Eiseley's allegorical essay "The World Eaters" recognizes man as a parasite who will consume until there is no more. Such insight serves as a "voice of warning" to all society of the types of possibilities of excesses featuring either too much isolation or civilization.

What humans can learn from isolation is self-reliance—they learn to make do with basics rather than luxuries, both intellectual and physical and the reward of which is intrinsic—"pride for having done so."

The other values Sayre lists are adventure—the value of discovery—of new lands, situations and cultures. Along with discovering an adventure comes a knowledge and understanding which allows men to see relationships more clearly—relationships with not only others of his kind or nature, but with himself. This understanding is in courage, friendship, death, fear and hunger; all of which are attributes defined for ages as desirable:

"Know thyself"—Socrates

"Control thyself"—Cicero

"Give thyself"—Christ

The only way to learn knowledge, control and selflessness is through experience and careful examination of it. This is the justification for climbing. As Sayre concludes, "Men climb mountains because they are not satisfied to exist, they want to live."

Woodrow Wilson Sayre

Douq Scott

*D*ouglas Kevin Scott was born to George Douglas and Edith Joyce Scott, 29 May 1941, in Nottingham, England. Little did Mr. and Mrs. Scott know that their son was to become one of the best and most prolific of all the world's mountaineers.

Doug Scott was educated at Cottesmore secondary school, Mundella Grammar School, and Nottingham Loughborough Teachers' Training College, graduating with a teaching certificate.

Scott's climbing career began at twelve years old on the local British crags. By the age of sixteen, he had traveled to the Alps and has continued to do so yearly.

Scott has many first ascents to his credits, ranging from the Alps to Yosemite, and from Alaska to the Himalayas.

Along with his activity in climbing Scott has also been an active contributer to the world of mountain literature. He has contributed numerous articles to **The Alpine Journal** (British), *The American Alpine Journal* and *Mountain Magazine.* He has published several books including: *Big Wall Climbing, Climbs on Derwent Valley Limestone,* and *Himalayan Climber.* Scott was editor of *Alpine Climbing* from 1971 to 1972 and is former president of the Alpine Climbing Group. Paradoxically Scott is at the same time a vegetarian and is an active rugby union player.

...to adapt and to survive.

Doug Scott

To Adapt and to Survive:

Douc Scott

Doug Scott's work "A Crawl Down the Ogre" is not among the class of "formal essays." Because of the personal narrative approach it fits more in with essays of an "informal" nature. One possible reason for Scott's informal approach may very possibly be due to when it was written. Even the world of literature has failed to escape the somewhat irreverent changes in decorum and propriety of the 20th Century. Scott, though university-educated, is much less "stuffy" than those early mountaineers, like Sir Leslie Stephen, who would be his Victorian equivalent. The early essayists seemed to write to a more educated elite whereas Scott seems to write to all who will read. From a transcendentalist's point of view Scott's might well be the most valid "chant" in that it seems to be more far-reaching.

With his informality Scott addresses many of the same issues spoken of by Hunt and Stephen and Gervasutti—he first of all recognizes the social microcosom the expedition team represents and in this particular case they represent a sort of Utopia as each member's expedition experience has allowed them each to transcend the need of one chosen leader:

> The expedition finally resolved itself into a party of six: Paul ('Tut') Braithwaite and I were to try the South Pillar, while Chris Bonington, Nick Estcourt, Mo Anthoine and Clive attempted the South-West Flank. We were, mercifully, without a leader, for the inclusion of such a personage would have been laughable, seeing that all members of the team had had so much expedition expe-

rience that they could easily arrive at decisions communally, with no bother at all. For some, this was their first leaderless expedition, and they no doubt found it stimulating to work things out for themselves, while former leaders perhaps found it restful to be without the burden of total responsibility. (Scott 231)

This example recommends to the reader that deference to individual experience is a key to social harmony whether in the scope of a limited expedition or on the larger scale of human society. In the competitive, credential-oriented society of today it is difficult and sometimes even threatening to give credit or recognition to the obvious strong abilities of others. Such an attitude feeds the need for leaders which sometimes infringes on the personal freedom of the individual.

For climbing, especially in isolated areas and with a small expedition the need for group strength as well as individual strength is of paramount importance not only to the success of the expedition but for actual physical survival. One important lesson that comes from climbing is that one learns what one's limitations are and that it is extremely important to face up to them. There is little or no room for egos in climbing. Scott illustrates this point very clearly by using as an example Chris Bonington's willingly turning over of the lead to Scott due to his physical condition.

Chris was feeling the effects of his previous attempt. He was moving well enough, but suggested that I led the rocks ahead, as I should be faster, being fitter. I greedily accepted and soon 'lost' myself climbing two 150 ft. pitches up a pinnacle and down its far side to a snow patch on the north side of the summit rocks. (Scott 231)

Such willing admission of weakness comes hard to men caught up in the "isms" of credential-oriented society, but for Bonington it was a realistic recognition of the moment. Bonington is a fine climber—at least as good as Scott, but more importantly he has control of his destiny and ego appears to play a much less important role in his life than it does with his average societal counterpart involved in daily business. Mountaineers do have credentials, and are respected for them, but in high-risk situations such matters become of much less importance.

If any particular messages come through Scott's essays stronger than others, two stand out. First, the lesson of realistically dealing with problems, and second, human's limitless ability to adapt. The essay's title "A Crawl Down the Ogre," as well as Scott's allegorical introduction about fragile eggs, serves to lead the reader into an amazing personal account about human tenacity and endurance in incredibly difficult circumstances and how individual strength and collective strength preserved life and provided success. As mentioned earlier the leaderless expedition worked because of individual talents working toward a common goal—the summit of Bainth Brakk—"The Ogre."

The climb of the Ogre came as the result of a dream—granted it is not the type of dream that would provide any great comfort or excite any strong response by most people, but to the climber the thought of climbing virgin rock on an unclimbed mountain, such a dream represents a powerful fantasy. For Doug Scott the 23,900 peak in the Karakoram Himalayan was such a dream. He calls it an "obsession." His obsession was cut short and nearly destroyed due to an early injury to his climbing partner Tut Braithwaite.

> Despite an apparent lack of organization, we had worked hard preparaing for our respective routes, but these well-made plans foundered in our case when a big rock smashed into Tut's leg at the start of our South Pillar route . . . . So ended a two-year obsession—an obsession which had caused me to catch my breath a few times at the thought of taking off to climb with just two climbing ropes and one back down to the ground. (Scott 232)

The climber's response to such exigencies is "mountain one, climbers none." This attitude exhibited early in the expedition and chronicled early in the essay illustrates the reality with which such individuals operate. Even when it meant the possible abandonment of his two years "obsession," which was based on his making his own way without being "clamped to other people's fixed ropes." For industrialized man, being "clamped" to other's ropes is the status quo. Technology has made it too easy for humans to fail to make their own way—to be content with following the crowd.

Climbing frees humans from societal commitments and allows their to push to higher physical, mental and spiritual limits. Scott's writing style allows the reader to feel, if not first-hand, at least vicariously both the exhilaration and depression of human struggles with nature and with themselves. He provides an almost logistical account of the mundane

Doug Scott   77 chores that goes along with any expedition. Just as he is paid off for such struggle with the deep beauty found only in remote wilds so also is his reader with Scott's ability to describe with vivid honesty the climber's reward. This approach to writing is very effective. It is much the same as John Muir's essays that contain great amounts of scientific description broken by poetic passages about America's wilderness. Muir's essays worked to create numerous national parks, likewise Scott's works provide some justification for the acitivity of climbing through the record of transcendent beauty:

> . . . Then only half an hour later, inside my tent supping hot tea, I looked out of the entrance as the sun set and decided that up there at 22,000 feet, watching that sun dipping down, silver lining strands of cloud strung out over Snow Lake and the Hispar Glacier beyond. Range after range of bristling mountain peaks stood out silhouetted against each other. The nearer ranges sharply and darkly defined, while those in the distance faded into the sun's diffuse haze of yellow light. Above them all, some hundred and fifty miles away, Nanga Parbat caught the last of the sun, whilst everywhere else was plunged into gloom. (Scott 233-234)

Man's need for security is also outlined: "We zipped up the tent against a strong wind and snuggled content into our feathers" (Scott 234).

The concept of human's adaptability to the most adverse of conditions is probably the most important message contained in this essay. Scott uses a personal experience of near tragedy to illustrate human ability to survive by his ability to adapt. This concept has both evolutionary and social implications. The "survival of the fittest" by "natural selection" is evident where, because of injury, Scott figuratively discards his uselessly broken lower legs and actually adapts and becomes efficient without them. Such illustration can be used as a social allegory, pointing out how to adapt and survive when part of the tools originally thought necessary to survive are taken away. This allegory became part of Scott's reality when his tools were lost when he was injured after having reached the top. On the descent, in darkness Scott slipped while rappelling diagonally down. Suddenly the game's rules were amended:

I leaned across to fix myself on to a peg, pressing myself over with my feet. I stepped my right foot up against the wall, but, in the gathering darkness, unwittingly placed it on a veneer of water ice. Suddenly my foot shot off and I found myself swinging away into the gloom, clutching the end of the rope. I couldn't imagine why the swing was going on and on. I had not realized how far left of the abseil sling I was. And all the time I was swinging, a little exclamation of awe, surprise and fear was coming out from inside me, audible to Mo some 2,000 ft. away at the snow-cave. And then the swing and the cry ended as I slammed into the opposite side of the gully, 100 ft. away. Splat! Glasses gone and every bone shaken. A quick examination revealed head and trunk O.K. femurs and knees O.K. but—Oh! Oh!—my ankles cracked whenever I moved them. The right one felt very peculiar: Pott's fracture, I diagnosed, without much real idea—left one, too, but perhaps it's just the tendons. So that was how it was going to be: a whole new game with new restrictions on winning—it was curious to observe my own reactions. I had no fear then, there was too much to do: I banged a peg in, put a couple of wire nuts in, tied off direct from my harness and hung off them while Chris came down the abseil rope.

"What ho!" he said, cheerily.

"I've broken my right leg and smashed the left ankle," I said.

"We'll just work at getting you down," he replied, airily. "Don't worry, you're a long way from death."

Too true!—the thought that I might have major problems of that kind had not then entered my head. I felt extremely rational, remarkably clear about what to do. (Scott 237-238)

Scott's evalution of his predicament is filled with his adoption of a philosophy summed up by "So that was how it was going to be: a whole new game with new restrictions on winning." This philosophy and self-evaluation in dealing with injury and fear is also reflected in his climbing partner, Chris Bonington's response to Scott's situation, "We'll work at getting you down—Don't worry, you're a long way from death." The only way to tackle such problems on the mountain—as well as anywhere else is one step at a time:

There was only one way for me to tackle a big complex problem like that, and that was one day at a time, keeping the broad idea hovering around in my mind that I'd got to get to Base Camp, but each day thinking no further than that day's objective, confident that if each day's climbing was competently executed then the whole problem would eventually be solved. (Scott 241)

It is interesting to note that even in such adverse and trying circumstances Scott still can see the beauty of wild nature: "At last the clouds were rolling back to reveal the mountains all around covered in fresh, sparkling snow down to the glaciers" (Scott 244).

Jose Vasconcelos, in his short story "The Boar Hunt" illustrates the mental escape that occurs even in desperate situations. This escape is the result of overpowering fatigue but serves as a source of renewal to not only the body but to the mind: "Fatigue over came us, that heavy fatigue which compels the soldier to scorn danger, to put down his rifle, and to fall asleep though the most persistent enemy pursues him." Such rest allows one to go on when things seem impossible—to overcome obstacles to survival:

I took many rests, flopping down flat out in the snow. Expeditions are usually good times to sort out a few things in the head—times to drop down a level or two—but it occured to me then that since my accident I had brought such an iron will to bear on every moment of the day that I had not given such matters a thought. But there had been some compensations, for whenever I shut my eyes I went off into a hallucinatory world of lilac and purple colouring, incredible shapes and forms, caricature people and stylised views of distant times and places. It did not make a lot of sense, but it was one way to while away a few minutes and recover enough to take a further twenty or so crawling paces through the snow. (Scott 244-245)

Scott's essay comes to an end with some interesting observations of a primitive society which like the expedition relied on individuals working in unison to produce a harmonious society.

In three days they carried me down to the Biafo Glacier and then along to its snout and then to a flat field near Askole, where a helicopter could land. It was a remarkable journey on a home-made stretcher constructed of juniper wood pole, a climbing rope and sleeping mats. Never once did they look like dropping me, and I seldom felt a jolt. It was good to lie out, listening and waiting as they made decisions as to route-finding, choice of camping place, who should fetch wood and water, who should take the heavier part of the stretcher, and so on. They inevitably made the decision after a gentle murmur had gone round the motley band— no one ever shouted or became excited. Their voices blended into a sing-song melody which seemed completely in tune with the rhythm of their village lives. They know just what to do. And I for one have nothing but admiration for these hardy people, who are all very individualistic and full of character, yet are easily capable of working to a common aim in complete accord. That is how good expeditions can work. (Scott 247-248)

This harmonious microcosm found both in the expedition and the Balti society is the very thing the adherents to transcendentalism see in nature which creates harmonious examples for the instruction of human society to use as models for themselves. It is ironic to find that a primitive, handmade stretcher can provide more security and comfort than can a helicopter, and that humans in the most wild environs can work and live with less stress, and more comfort, than found in the world's most modern cities.

The Machapuchare

Arlene Blum

Arlene Blum

$\mathcal{A}$rlene Blum, currently the world leader in women's climbing, started her career in 1963 and since that time has reached the pinnacle of women's mountaineering. She has led numerous all-women's expeditions, including the 1978 successful expedition to Annapurna, which also set the North American altitude record for women. Blum participated in the 1974 International Pamirs expedition and had led the first all woman ascent of Alaska's Mount McKinley. Blum has led or participated in fifteen high altitude expeditions.

Blum received her undergraduate degree from Reed College and her Ph.D. from the University of California at Berkeley. Her scholarly achievements are as impressive as her climbing achievements. She is a distinguished chemical researcher and has taught and done research at U.C. Berkeley, Stanford University, M.I.T. and Wellesley College. She is an active lecturer and has published widely.

Blum has received numerous awards including the Sierra Club's Francis P. Farquar mountaineering award and the Society of Women Geographers Gold Medal.

On Annapurna, with Machapuchare over the clouds.

Arlene Blum

Reaffirmation of Life:

Arlene Blum

*A*rlene Blum is one of the most poetic and is among the most insightful of climber/writers. Unlike the others, with the somewhat limited exception of Herzog's nationalism, Blum views the expedition as a political tool—a vehicle to promote the issues of the women's movement. Yet she is not over-zealous by any means. If anything, she is subtle and very sensitive to the messages that are to be had from exploring wild nature, and even more sensitive to the value and quality of human life. From her book *Annapurna: A Woman's Place*, entitled "The Memorial," is the account of the expedition after its initial success of seeing two of its members reach the summit of Annapurna as well as the tragedy of losing two members in a climbing accident. Herein Blum discusses many of the previously discussed concepts of community, of risk and beauteous nature, but she does it with a different type of poetic sensitivity—one that the reader responds to much differently than he or she does to other previous essays. One factor that allies Blum to the mountain writers of the nineteenth century is that she has to provide the reader with some sort of justification for why women would leave the security of domestic and professional life to risk life and limb to climb some mountain that most of the rest of the world doesn't even know exists. In this sense she is no different from Stephen, Mummery and Tyndall, for they too had to justify the climbing of mountains to their readers. Blum does this with her descriptions of the wonders of the Himalaya and with her sensitive reflections on the overall good of such activities. On the other hand, Blum is very modern because she is able to deal with the pressures, not only of leadership of an expedition which, as mentioned before, was paradoxically both successful and tragic; but she is not afraid to express emotion. Blum, with a particular feminine sensitivity, deals with emotions brought on by experiences created by the expedition that is best expressed by male writers of earlier times in a descriptive or lyrical passage dealing with mountain splendor. Her writing is honest, and real because she recognizes emotion, not as weakness, but as a normal function of human beings. Another aspect of her honesty is found in the profound sadness that shows through when she is speaking about her lost comrades.

In previous chapters it has been stated that the most valuable reward found in climbing is the intrinsic—the transcendent harmony of man and nature. Reading about the injury of Scott described in "Crawl Down the Ogre" one wonders if the trancendent "high" is somewhat diminished. If it is, even in the slightest degree by mere injury, it would then be reasonable to say that death would totally destroy it. This argument has come from both those with actual first-hand experience as well as from those who read only sketchy newspaper accounts of dead climbers. Yet it appears that Blum skillfully reconciles this apparent paradox by combining her account of the physical effort required for mere existence at high altitude, which has made worthwhile the victory of the summit, and the irreversible loss of two team mates:

> The time had come to take down the colorful tents at Camp II that had sheltered us over these past weeks. Was it only weeks? It seemed as if we had lived up here for a very long time. Christy and I packed up huge loads—at least 70 pounds—and stumbled down the glacier in the hot sun. Now that the climb was over, the air was calm and the mountain looked sunny and benign. I could not help glancing up from time to time to the serac near Camp IV where I knew Alison and Vera were. (Blum 261)

Her treatment of victory and loss is much like the self psychotherapy of Hemingway's fiction, "The Way You'll Never Be" and "The Big Two Hearted River," upon his return from World War I. He returned physically wounded and mentally broken, yet through his writing he manages to heal both his body and mind. Blum's reactions to her lost friends illustrates Freud's theories as in *Civilization and Its Discontents*: denial, then anger, then remorse, followed by realization and acceptance. The Freudian method is expressed, but in a shortened version by the

Arlene Blum

Sherpa Lopsang: "Let them go. You have to let them go" (Blum 261). Yet the awful reality returns each time she looks at the seracs near Camp IV where still is visible the red of the fallen comrade's parka against the stark whiteness of the snow.

The actual physical activities of breaking camp and moving down the mountain serve as a means to force the recognition and finally the acceptance of the lost members' deaths: "Each step into the gray, muffling fog took us farther from Annapurna, from Vera and Alison. Each step brought us closer to the reality that they were not coming with us. Occasionally I felt waves of elation that we had actually succeeded, had reached the top of Annapurna, but mostly I was filled with despair" (Blum 261-262).

Like Geoffrey, the main character in D.H. Lawrence's "*Love Among the Hay Stacks*," who goes through this same progression of mourning, Blum still has gained some strong spiritual enlightenment and this essay represents the "Chant." The enlightened return from ideality is not always happy, but it does lead to a "higher conduct of life." This point is again clearly illustrated by David Robert's essay "Mountain of My Fear," where he too after reaching the summit of Huntington in Alaska has his victory somewhat clouded by the deaths of his two partners. Even in the face of tragedy, like Blum he nevertheless finds himself better off—uplifted by the communion with wild nature.

Throughout this study the point has been made that human ability to reason has made them the most adaptable of creatures. Blum supports this idea, as she justified Piro's decision to retreat from attempting to summit the Annapurna, due to the possible outcome i.e., permanent damage to her hands. This also reveals how physically fragile the human being is:

Throughout the day the rest of the team members and Sherpas straggled down to base camp with enormous packs. Piro arrived with her finger still heavily bandaged, but she was confident it would heal and that she could continue to perform surgery. What an enormous difference such a small thing as a tear in a glove can make. Had it not been for that small hole, Piro would certainly have made the summit. (Blum 263)

Here Blum again illustrates how unforgiving wilderness can be by her realization that the most apparently insignificant accident in such a hostile environment can dash hopes, and sometimes, bring about dis-aster. She does this by referring to the tear in Piro's glove. The point is made that even with all the glories of wild nature there still exists an enormous indifference, indifference in the form of avalanches, cold and other hazards that can destroy a human being in seconds. Another reality clearly expressed by Blum which the other writers have also rec-ognized is that humans are social animals—that humans are strongest in number particularly when there is a common goal and each of the number contribute to its realization.

> Soon the team was together again at Base Camp. Looking up at the remote summit, it was hard to believe that any of us had ever stood there, even harder to comprehend the great loss that accom-panied our achievement. But we had gained something more than the summit. The years of planning and the months of climbing together had changed and strengthened us. We had survived the hardest physical and psychological stresses and found that as a team we could do great things. Each woman had contributed her abilities and effort in full measure, and each was rewarded with the knowledge that her contribution had helped us attain our goal. In addition, we had gained the friendship and warmth that now united us. The long-standing conflict between Joan and me had been amicably resolved, and no other lasting antagonisms had de-veloped during the past stress-filled months. For me, this was as important as having reached the summit. (Blum 264)

While Blum deals with the similarities of this expedition—(or any expedition for that matter) she walks the reader through her process of mourning. She does this by continually referring back to her dead friends and the obligations connected with their deaths as expedition leader. Each reference takes the reader through her healing process, beginning with her initial grief and sorrow each time she retraced the expedition's progress toward the summit, the letters to the families of the dead, the putting off of the memorial service and the creation of the monument:

> During the course of the day we all took turns chipping the letters of Vera's and Alison's names in the memorial stone. We had planned to hold a memorial service that afternoon, but kept putting it off, fearing the finality of it. At last, when it was almost dark

and the summit shrouded in fog, we could wait no longer; we would be breaking camp early the next day. We walked over to the rock in the somber twilight and stood there silently. Our minds and hearts were filled with thoughts of Vera and Alison, but we could not say anything. (Blum 268)

Part of the mourning process when connected with climbing deaths calls for some sort of justification. Blum's justification comes as well-thought-out and realistic ideas on risk. Each member of the expedition knew from the onset of the risks involved because they had previous experience with what possibilities they would be faced with:

Vera and Alison, like all high-altitude climbers, had taken risks in the mountains before. Vera had told us many stories of her solo climb of Aconcagua: of severe storms, hallucinations, the horror of finding a boot with a human leg bone in it. Still she had persevered, climbing all the way to the top and back down by herself. And Alison, while climbing Noshaq in 1972, had been part of a team that elected to continue onto the top in the late afternoon, even though they knew that the descent would be hazardous in the dark. Coming down, Alison lost her crampon, fell, and stopped herself just in time above a cliff. But this time neither she nor Vera had been so fortunate. (Blum 265)

But also with the knowledge of the possibilites of disaster was the knowledge of the reward which is the thing that drives people to adventure which Blum calls a "reaffirmation of life:"

When I had crossed the avalanche slope for the last time, I felt myself on a distinct edge: on one side was the abyss of falling snow, burial, death; on the other side was life and a renewed appreciation of its value. Those weeks spent under the threat of imminent death—followed by the loss of Vera and Alison—had taught us to see the important things, to focus on essentials. We had risked our lives, and our reward was in part a reaffirmation of life. (Blum 271)

Humans have been tireless in seeking ways to make life better, more rewarding. This desire is common in humanity—it is found in current societies considered primitive by western standards. The backward peoples build, trade, teach and pray in hopes of making life better—by doing things that will leave a mark on history and hopefully elevate those who follow. Blum's expedition did just that as is expressed in the words of Marquita Maytag, the American Ambassador to Nepal: "What a wonderful thing you have done for yourselves and for the women of the world" (Blum 238). These women climbers have made a timeless contribution not only to women but to all humans. It is just as timeless as the rock monument that holds the photographs and bears the names of Vera Watson and Alison Chadwick who died for it:

> When everyone else had left, I went and sat by the memorial stone a last time. I touched Vera's and Alison's names and tried to focus on the happier times of the last months. I rembered Vera playing with the puppy on the trek, Alison's and Liz's delight when they established Camp I, the joy of the summit, the ethereal beauty of this world of rock, ice, and snow. And then I thought of the migrating geese, which had been flying back and forth between Tibet and India since before the Himalaya had been uplifted and would continue to do so long after we were all forgotten. (Blum 271-272)

In the end, Blum discovered her own understanding:

"In mountaineering, the truism holds: the greatest rewards come only from the greatest commitment. On Annapurna our entire team took the risk, made the commitment." (Blum 275)

On the South Face of the Annapurna.

Arlene Blum

David Roberts

*D*avid Roberts is recognized for his ability to write about wilderness and wilderness activity. His books *Deborah: A Wilderness Narrative, Moments of Doubt* and *The Mountain of My Fear* were acclaimed by W.H. Auden as "excellent books." He has published numerous articles and essays in **Outside, National Geographic**, and **Smithsonian** magazines and was one of a select group of mountain essayists asked to contribute to Michael Tobias' and Harold Dragdo's excellent collection entitled *Mountain Spirit.*

Educated as an undergraduate at Harvard in mathemtics, he then went on to the University of Denver where he received his Ph.D. in English.

His wilderness and mountaineering activities include: Director of the Outdoors Program at Hampshire College, Instructor for both the Adirondack Institute and Outward Bound.

Roberts has climbed extensively in Alaska, including first ascent of the west face of Mount Huntington, the first big wall climbed in the Great Gorge of the Ruth Glacier. He has climbed and explored the Revelation Mountains, the Cathedral Spires, and the Brooks Range. He has climbed the Wickersham Wall of Mount McKinley.

David Roberts

The Irony of Existence:

David Roberts

*F*or David Roberts the question of "why?" is immediately answered: climbing provides the room in life to find answers. The answers come in the form of some type of spiritual or intellectual enlightenment. The question one must ask is: "Does this enlightenment that comes from wilderness experience always represent a happy or euphoric enlightenment or it may come despite great cost—mental and/or physical suffering, pain and even death?" After reading Herzog's or Scott's accounts of their wild experiences one would have to answer "Yes," to the latter question: Sometimes the knowledge does come at great cost—terrible physical pain and tremendous mental suffering but always there is the heightened return to the social world.

In Roberts' essay as well as in Blum's the physical suffering found in Herzog's and Scott's accounts is noticeably absent. Aside from the tremendous physical effort it takes to travel at great heights, nothing is mentioned about frostbite and amputations or less conventional forms of locomotion such as crawling with broken legs. But what Roberts and Blum both discuss is the most final of all consequences attached to risky activities—death. Can there be any good come from an expedition where there is loss of life?

Roberts deals with the concept of community isolation but in a different way. In his aloneness nearing the summit of Huntington he recognizes a scrap of human litter as a testament to man's persistence—his desire to constantly push himself toward the pinnacle of existence; he readily attaches himself to the French rope, though useless. He sees this as a form of security—not so much in the literal sense but figuratively. By this act he becomes part of greater humanity—he is hanging on to all of human history.

> As I neared the bottom of the first wall, I thought I saw something sticking out of the snow. I climbed over to it. Stretched tight in the air, a single, frail foot of thin rope emerged from the ice. I pulled on it, but it was stuck solid. The sight was strangely moving. It testified, in a way, both to the transicence and to the persistence of man. That bit of French fixed rope was the only human thing not our own that we have found during the whole expedition. It even seemed to offer a little security. I clipped in to it although I knew it was probably weather-rotten. (Roberts 286)

The form of this essay follows that of the informal rather than formal approach in that it is a personal narrative. Its tone somehow is less upbeat—less alluring than the others. It seems to be darker in tone which adds to, though by implication, the original question about the experience of enlightenment mentioned earlier. The very title "The Mountain of My Fear" shows this.

Roberts, in his approach to this essay, recognizes the transcendental quality of reaching the summit and discusses the actual beautiful vision that comes from standing on one of earth's high places. Yet before he describes the beauty he, almost as if to prepare the reader for the dark outcome of his report, mentions that he and his party were really too tired to really enjoy their victory and restates it after his description of beauty:

> It was 3:30 a.m. We'd been going for sixteen hours without rest. Now we were too tired even to exalt. The sun had just risen in the northeast; a hundred and thirty miles away we could see Deborah, only a shadow in the sky. As Don looked at it I said, "This makes up for a lot." He nodded. . . If only this moment could last, I thought, if no longer than we do. But what I should remember would be the memories themselves, rehearsed like an archaic dance; that I should stare at the pcitures and try to get back inside them, reaching out for something that had slipped out of my hands and spilled in the darkness of the past. And that someday I might be so old that all that might pierce my senility would be the vague heart-pang of something lost and inexplicably sacred,

maybe not even the name Huntington meaning anything to me, nor the names of three friends, but only the precious sweetness leaving its faint taste mingled with the bitter of one dying. And that there were only four of us (four is not many), and that surely within eighty years and maybe within five (for climbing is dangerous) we would all be dead, the last of our death closing a legacy not even the mountain itself could forever attest to. (Roberts 287-288)

Like all mountain writers, when dealing with the question of "Why humans climb?" Roberts first of all sees the summit as a microcosm of human existence isolated from the rest of society, as a place where one can truly examine others without all the interruptions and "What ifs" of society. He recognizes the relative nature of the summit victory as being somewhat paradoxical in that it has been achieved by community effort, yet he knows how fragile that effort is and how individual dreams and desires, if known to others, could have thwarted the victory. Humans in numbers are strong but not omnipotent. Roberts recognizes the ability of individual will to crush collective will.

I wanted to know how the others felt and couldn't. Trying to talk about it now would have seemed profane; if there was anything we shared, it was the sudden sense of quiet and rest. For each of us, the high place we had finally reached culminated ambitions and secret desires we could scarcely have articulated had we wanted to. And the chances are our various dreams were different. If we had been able to know each others' perhaps we could not have worked so well together. Perhaps we would have recognized, even in our partnership, the vague threats of ambition, like boats through a fog: the unrealizable desires that drove us beyond anything we could achieve, that drove us in the face of danger; our unanswerable complaints against the universe—that we die, that we have so little power, that we are locked apart, that we do not know. So perhaps the best things that happened on the summit were what we could see happening, not anything beneath. (Roberts *289*)

Roberts also seems to see the irony of human existence—collectively as well as individually. Humans can have and have had tremendous impact on the natural world—they have saved and protected nature, but they have knowingly plundered it as well. One irresponsible individual can, on a motorcycle, do more damage to an alpine meadow in twenty minutes that nature with all its forces can in several hundred years. Yet the summit of Huntington revealed to the four climbers human frailty. After their persistent effort to reach it, it "looked no different than when we had come, but for the faint footprints we had left near it" (Roberts 290).

Roberts, aside from his mention of aloneness, very early in the essay referring to the French rope says little more about it until he deals with the death of Ed, his climbing partner while they are descending in the dark. It is somewhat ironic that they would risk descending in darkness because of the relative discomfort of sharing a small tent with the other two members of their party. Climbers pride themselves on the ability to endure hardships. Yet it was for creature comforts that this risk is taken. It almost seems contradictory for a climber, who willingly braves cold and other physical discomfort, not to mention mental and social discomfort, would take unneeded risk for more sleeping space and extra food, yet they did. This probably gives some indication that altitude and fatigue as well as stress clouds the ability to reason clearly.

In dealing with the expedition tragedy, Roberts, without emotion, (at least emotion as is illustrated in Blum's essay), faces reality: "I knew when he had fallen there wasn't a chance of his stopping for 4,000 feet" (Roberts 293). The thing that makes this account so powerful is Roberts's sudden recognition of aloneness due to the silence: "I became aware of the acute silence. All I could hear was the sound of water dripping near me" (Roberts 293). It is the awesome silence—a silence that is only found in the most remote places that serves as the illustration of the danger of isolation and human instinctual fear of it.

Isolation, as discussed before with the illustration from Conrad's *Heart of Darkness*, is dangerous because it makes people do things that they normally would not do. Kurtz becomes more savage than the savages of the wild jungle, whereas Roberts' almost risks his own life by seeking the company of others:

> I tried to shout for help to Matt and Don. But they were nearly 1,000 feet above, hidden by cliffs that deflected and snow that absorbed my voice. I realized they couldn't hear me. Even the echo of my shouts in the dark seemed tiny. I couldn't just stand

there; either I must go up or I must go down. It was about an equal distance either way, but the pitches above were more difficult. I had no rope. There was no point going up, because there was nothing we could do for Ed. His body lay now, as far as anyone could ever know, on the lower Tokositna, inaccessible. An attempt even by the three of us to descend the 4,000 feet to look for him would be suicidally dangerous, especially since we would have only one rope for all of us. If I went up, I should eventually have to go down again. All it could do was add to the danger. I realized these things at the time. Yet the instinct, in my isolation, to try to join Matt and Don was so compelling that for a while I didn't even consider the other possibility. But it became obvious I had to go down. (Roberts 294)

Another irony that appears at this point is found in the way Ed dies. Roberts alludes to the possibility of mechanical failure—broken carabiner or rappel device or at least misuse. According to Bonnatti one of the reasons men in the twentieth century go to the mountains is to escape the over-technical "mechanical" existence society has lapsed into: "All that mattered was that our perfect expedition, in one momentary mechanical whim, had turned into a trial of fear and sorrow" (296-297). It is ironic that in an attempt to get close to wilderness and to be away from civilization that men rely on mechanical devices to do so and that sometimes these trusted devices fail.

In an attempt to "salvage" something from the death of Ed, Roberts fell back upon memories:

Already I had begun to miss Ed in a way separate from the shock and loneliness. I longed for his cheeriness, that fund of warmth that Matt, Don, and I lacked. I had wanted so much to relax in the tent, talking and joking with him, reliving the long summit day. I hadn't climbed with him since July 11. Now it was the last day of the month, and he was gone.

I tried to relive every moment Ed and I had had together the last day, as if doing so could somehow salvage something from the tragedy. My recollections had stuck on a remark he had made in the Nose Camp as we rested after the summit. I had told him that it had been the best day I'd ever had climbing. Ed had said, "Mine too, but I don't know if I'd do the whole thing again." (Roberts 297)

Ed's thought about the expedition and the fact that Ed climbed less than the other members represents a sort of cruel injustice. Life too is full of this sort of injustice as William Faulkner said: "It's the irrevocability of action that is tragic." Faulkner's short story "Tomorrow" reinforces the reality of injustice in life. Roberts looks for ways to rectify the mountain tragedy:

Now his remark haunted me. The accident, ultimately inexplicable beyond its mechanical cause, which itself we would never be sure of, seemed that much more unfair in view of what Ed had said. It would have been better, fairer, perhaps, had it happened to me. Yet not even in the depth of anguish could I wish that I had died instead. And that irreducible selfishness seemed to prove to me that beyond our feeling of "commitment" there lay the barriers of our disparate self-love. We were willing to place our lives in each other's hands, but I wouldn't have died for Ed. What a joke we played on ourselves—the whole affair of mountaineering seemed a farce then. But the numbness returned; I told myself to wait to judge it all in better perspective, months, years from now. (Roberts 299-300)

Here Roberts is honest, starkly honest, as he presents his realization that everyone is locked into self. This may be an allusion to his possible existentialism. Despite the community of the mountain, this fundamental isolation is brought out by the encounter with savage nature and inexplicable death.

As the days passed and after being reunited with his friends Roberts attempts to justify the loss in historical terms by calling to mind other "small" expeditions that had incurred death as part of the outcome. It's hard enough to justify to the average member of society why men climb and its even harder to justify death:

I thought of how rarely an expedition is both successful and tragic, especially a small expedition. Something like 95 per cent of the danger in a climb such as ours lay in the ascent. But we had worked for thirty-one days, many of them dangerous, on the route without a serious injury before finally getting to the summit. Going down should have taken only two or three days, and it is usually routine to descend pitches on which fixed ropes have been left. I was reminded of the first ascent of the Matterhorn, when only hours after its conquest the climbing rope broke, sending four of Edward Whymper's seven-man party to their deaths. Then I realized that the Matterhorn had been climbed one hundred years, almost to the day, before our ascent. I thought, also, of the ascent of Cerro Torre in Patagonia in 1959, still regarded by many as the hardest climb ever done. On its descent Toni Egger, one of the best mountaineers in the world, had fallen off a cold rappel to his death, leaving only Cesare Maestri to tell of their victory. But thinking of those climbs explained ours no better. I knew that Whymper, after the Matterhorn, had been persecuted by the public, some of whom even suggested he had cut the rope. I knew that, even in an age that understands mountaineering a little better than the Victorians did, vague suspicions still shrouded the Cerro Torre expedition. But even if we could explain Ed's death to mountaineers, how could we ever explain it to those who cared more about him than about any mountain? (Roberts 301-302)

The image of the "Hero" in modern society is strange. If a man or woman does something exciting, risky, or adventuresome and succeeds they become "Heroes." If they fail and die as a result they are stupid and irresponsible. Yet how easily countries ship young men off to war, which unlike exploring, which is a celebration of life at its fullest, has as its purpose to kill or be killed. The argument against mountaineering has been always present even from the beginning. One particular case, possibly the most famous for attacking mountaineering because of lost life is that of Edward Whymper's "broken rope" after the first ascent of the Matterhorn, where while descending four climbers were killed. Roberts makes reference to this incident, but more interestingly is Anthony Trollope's essay "A Further Defence," where he defends Whymper as well as climbing in general. Trollope's argument is timeless as it is just as relevant today as when it was written. In order to do it justice, "A Further Defense" appears at length:

> It would have been easier and much pleasanter to write of the Alpine Club man, and to describe his peculiarities and his glories, if that terrible accident had not happened on the Matterhorn. It is

ill jesting while the sad notes of some tragic song are still sounding in our ears. But the Alpine Club man has of late made himself so prominent among English tourists,—has become, with his ropes, his blankets, and his ladders, so well-acknowledged and much-considered an institution, that it would be an omission were he not to be included in our sketches. And, moreover, it may not be amiss to say yet a word or two as to the dangers of Alpine Club pursuits,—a word or two to be added to all those words that have been said in these and other columns on the same subject.

It may well, I think, be made a question whether we are not becoming too chary of human life; whether we do not allow ourselves to be shocked beyond proper measure by the accidental death of a fellow mortal. There are two points of view from which we look at these sudden strokes of fate, which are so distinctly separated in our minds as to turn each calamity into two calamities; and the one calamity or the other will be regarded as the more terrible according to the religious tendencies of the suffering survivor. There is the religious point of view, which teaches us to consider it to be a terrible thing that a man should be called upon to give up his soul without an hour for special preparation; and there is the human point of view, which fills us with an ineffable regret that one well loved him, apparently without a cause. . . . As regards the religious consideration, we know of course that we are constantly praying, with more or less of earnestness, that the evil of sudden death may not come upon us, as we pray also that battles may not come. But yet, if occasion require it, if the honour of the country seems to demand it, we do not hesitate about battles. We may say, at least, that we never hesitate with extreme caution on the score of the money that must be spent.

And we consider,—if the cause has been good,—that the blood spilt on battle-fields has been well spilt, and that the lives gallantly rendered there have been well rendered. But the carnage there has all been the carnage of sudden death. It may be,—and yet it may hardly be,—that the soldier, knowing the chances of his profession, shall keep himself prepared for the death-dealing blow; but if the soldier on the eve of battle can do so, then why not he who is about to climb among the mountain snows? But, in truth, the subject is one which does not admit of too curious an inquiry. As we pray to be removed from sudden death, so do we pray that we may always be prepared for it. We are going ever with our lives in our hands, knowing that death is common to all of us; and knowing also,—for all of us who ever think do know it,—that to him who dies death must be horrible or blessed, not in accordance with an hour or two of final preparation, but as may be the state of the dying man's parting soul as the final result of the life which he has led. It suits us in some of our religious moods to insist much on the special dangers of sudden death, but they are dangers which come home in reality to very few of us. . . In war, in commerce, not unfrequently in science, we disregard utterly the perils of sudden death; and if, as regards religion, these perils do not press on us in war and commerce, or in science, neither should they do so in reference to other pursuits. Is there any man with a faith so peculiar as to believe that salvation will be refused to him who perishes among the mountains of Europe because his employment is regarded as an amusement; but that it will be given to the African traveller because his work is to be accounted as a work of necessity? For myself, I do not think that there is a man who so believes.

And as to the human point of view,—that wearing regret which almost melts the heart into a stream of woe when the calamity comes home to oneself,—the argument is nearly the same. The poor mother whose dear gallant boy has fallen in battle . . . cannot reconcile herself to the need of war, nor unless she be a Spartan, can she teach herself to think that that dear blood has been well shed for the honour of her country. And, should he have fallen from some snowy peak, her judgment of the event will be simply the same. It will be personal regret, not judgment. It is equally impossible that she should console herself in either event by calculating that the balance of advantage to the community of which she is a member is on that side to which courage and the spirit of adventure belong.

In our personal regrets we must all think of our individual cases; but in discussing such a question as belonging to England at large, we can only regard the balance of advantage. And if we find that that spirit of enterprise which cannot have its full swing, or attain its required momentum without the fatality which will attend danger, leads to happy results,—that it makes our men active, courageous, ready in resource, prince to friendship, keen after gratifications which are in themselves good and noble; that it leads to pursuits which are in themselves lovely, and to modes of life which are worthy of admiration, then let us pay the necessary cost of such happy results without repining. That we should, all of us, have a tear of sorrow for those gallant fellows who perished on the Matterhorn is very good;—For Lycidas is dead, dead ere his prime, Young Lycidas, and hath not left his peer:

Who would not sing for Lycidas?

But shall it be said among us that no boat is again to be put off from our shores because that one "fatal and perfidious bark" was "built in the eclipse."

There is a fate infinitely worse than sudden death,—the fate of him who is ever fearing it. "Mors omnibus est communis." We all know it, and it is the excitement coming from that knowledge which makes life pleasant to us. When we hear of a man who is calm and collected under every danger, we know that we hear of a happy man. In hunting, in shooting, in yachting, in all adventures, in all travelling,—I had almost said in love-making itself,—the cream of the charm lies in the danger. But danger will not be danger long if none of the natural results of danger come; and the cream of such amusements would, under such safe circumstances, soon become poor and vapid as skim-milk. I would say that it is to be hoped that that accident on the Matterhorn may not repress the adventurous spirit of a single English mountain-climber, did I not feel so sure that there will be no such repression as to leave no room for hoping. . . .(Trollope 60-62)

Objectivity is the way to the issue. Sometimes one must stand way back in order to see clearly which allows one to see the whole context.

David Roberts

Sheldon kept saying, "Boy, that's rough. What happened?" All I could do was explain the facts of the accident. I couldn't explain beyond that; I couldn't tell him the urgency of our happiness before. Huntington faded behind us; I couldn't explain. We had spent forty days alone there, only to come back one man less, it seemed. We had found no answers to life: perhaps only the room in which to look for them. (Roberts 304)

The "Chant" isn't always pleasant or euphoric. Sometimes it's bitter and sad but regardless of its tone it is its message the "parcel of truth" that is its profundity.

David Roberts

Albert Fredrick Mummery

A. F. Mummery was born in Dover, Kent in 1855 a sickly child. He had permanent eye problems for the rest of his life.

Mummery had without doubt great influence on the world of Alpine climbing for two reasons: his many climbs and his farsighted philosophy. Mummery was a pioneer in guideless climbing and solo climbing.

He began his climbing career in 1871 but his great achievements began in 1878 when he took up with guide Alexander Burgener. In 1895, just prior to his leaving on his first and only trip to the Himalayas, his classic work *My Climbs in the Alps and Caucasus* was published. The last chapter of his work (and the one contained in this study) presents Mummery's philosophy of climbing and provided a lead for the future of the sport.

Upon his arrival in the Himalayas it was decided by Mummery and his climbing mate to attempt Nanga Parbat on which Mummery was killed.

Albert Fredrick Mummery

Climbing as Education:

A.F. Mummery

"The Pleasures and Penalties of Mountaineering" by A. F. Mummery directly attacks the argument that surrounds mountain climbing. With this clear and unabashed treatise Mummery discusses very objectively the concepts of risk, challenge, first hand experience, standards, psychology and provides his philosophy as to why humans climb.

Mummery sees climbing first and foremost as an educational process—a problem-solving process. Mummery states; "Indeed, if we consider the essence of the sport of mountaineering, it is obvious that it consists, and consists exclusively, in pitting the climber's skill against the difficulties opposed by the mountain" (Mummery 321). This is the process of life. Humans must learn to deal with the problems of existence; and if they fail to develop the skills needed to deal with those problems then their progress is stopped and they slough off. This principle of "natural selection" is dramatized in the art of rock climbing in that the climber is not content to overcome the same problems time after time but is always looking for new and more difficult problems: "The essence of the sport lies not in ascending a peak, but struggling with and overcoming difficulties. . .which tax to the utmost limits the powers of the mountaineers engaged" (Mummery 322). It is the struggle that makes humans strong. Doug Scott's example of problem solving is an excellent illustration of humans adapting to a situation—one that to most seems impossible—and coming out the winner.

In order to continue to develop and progress the individual must develop a sense of daring—they must be willing to deal with risk—to look at it logically and weigh the outcome compared to the loss:

To set one's utmost faculties, physical and mental, to fight some grim precipice, or force some gaunt, ice-clad gully, is work worthy of men; to toil up long slopes of screes behind a guide who can "lie in bed and picture every step of the way up with all the places for hand and foot," is work worthy of the fibreless contents of fashionable clothes, dumped with all their scents and ointments, starched linen and shiny boots, at Zermatt by the railway.

In other words, the true mountaineer is the man who attempts new ascents. Equally, whether he succeeds or fails, he delights in the fun and jollity of the struggle. The gaunt, bare slabs the square, precipitous steps in the ridge, and the black, bulging ice of the gully, are the very breath of life to his being. I do not pretend to be able to analyze this feeling, still less to be able to make it clear to unbelievers. It must be felt to be understood, but it is potent to happiness and sends the blood tingling through the veins, destroying every trace of cynicism and striking at the very roots of pessimistic philosophy. (Mummery 322-323)

This philosophy is much the same as that espoused by Henry David Thoreau in his essay entitled "Walking," where Thoreau proclaims the nobility of the Saunterer—the "holy-lander," one who is seeking the essence, the truth of existence. This concept of truth may come in different individual forms. For some it is the great transcendental vision which can be realized with little effort (though usually it comes only after much expense) or it can come to the euphoria found in the endorphin highs of the long distance runner:

It is possible, nay even probable, that much of the pleasure of mountaineering is derived from the actual physical effort and from the perfect state of health to which this effort brings its votaries, and, to this extent, may plausibly be alleged to be the mere sequence and development of the pole and tree climbing of our youth. (Mummery 323-324)

An excellent illustration of this concept is found in an article entitled "Risky Business" by Martin Begley in the May 1986 **Backpacker** magazine. This article discusses a new psychological theory propounded by Dr. Frank Farley of the University of Wisconsin-Madison who is involved in research dealing with "thrill seekers." He calls them "T" type personalities. One who fits into this "T" type category and who illustrates Mummery's position is John Roskelley, one of the premiere alpinists in the world. To him climbing combines attaining both the physical and mental maximum, then coming off it. "To reach a certain level of fear, sweat, maximum muscle breakdown—mental breakdown, at times—and see what you can do under extreme stress, under conditions you put yourself in" (38). To some it seems that anyone who would place themselves in such risky predicaments as climbers do is by no means able to partake of the aesthetic pleasures. This attitude comes from a faulty, preconceived notion—one of rationalization of inactivity and one which Mummery attacks:

> But why should a man be assumed incapable of enjoying aesthetic pleasures because he is also capable of the physical and non-aesthetic pleasures of rock climbing?

> A well-known mountaineer asserts that the fathers of the craft did not regard "The over-coming of physical obstacles by means of muscular exertion and skill" as "the chief pleasure of mountaineering.". . .Those who are so completely masters of their environment that they can laugh and rollick on the ridges, free from all constraint of ropes or fear of danger, are far more able to appreciate the glories of the "eternal hill" than those who can only move in constant terror of their lives, amidst the endless chapter and rank tobacco smoke of unwashed guides. (Mummery 324-325).

Mummery predicts the modern climbers who now wish to pit only themselves—free from any mechanical protection—against the mountain in search of the ultimate freedom and affirmation of life which includes an appreciation of the aesthetics as illustrated by John Bachar:

> I like to feel I'm in complete control up there. Every now and then I get a little scared, a little strung out, and have to do some moves I don't want to do, and that's not good. I like to feel super-solid, like I could just throw a little ballet on top of the whole thing. I can say I soloed this 5.12 or something, but that's not what really counts. It's how it felt. Some of the hard climbs I've soloed were maybe impressive from the outside, but inside I might not feel that great about them, because I was maybe only 90 per-

cent in control, and that's less than I want when I solo, because one move. . .I mean, you blow it once. . ."He'd hesitated, and I finished his sentence for him: ". . .the punishment is severe." (Begley; **Backpacker Magazine**, may 1986:116)

Dr. George Sheehan in his book *Running and Being*, states that even if medical research found that running was physically bad for him, he would continue to run because of the mental benefits he sees that it produces, which is a somewhat distant echo of Mummery's view of climbing. Mummery, like Roskelley today, loves the physical benefits of climbing and sees them as justification enough for risk, let alone the aesthetic benefits:

> I am free to confess that I myself should still climb, even though there were no scenery to look at, even if the only climbing attainable were the dark and gruesome pot-holes of the Yorkshire dales. On the other hand, I should still wander among the upper snows, lured by the silent mists and the red blaze of the setting sun, even though physical or other infinity, even though in after aeons the sprouting of wings and other angelic appendages may have sunk all thought of climbing and cragsmanship in the whelming past.(Mummery 325-326)

Mummery's philosophy of climbing as education must be looked at in the same way liberal education is structured today. The primary and secondary schools as well as the undergraduate college education provide basic skills required to move on to the specialty areas of the graduate schools where the previously learned skills are honed and sharpened—purified. In mountaineering the same process takes place in the same sequence of steps until the end, the reward is reached. In the introduction to this work, John Muir's experience on Mount Ritter is mentioned in part as an illustration of a transcendent experience related to man's physical ascent of a rock wall. It represents all the aspects Mummery ascribes to climbing, i.e., risk, experience, developed skills, challenge and reward. The reward is two fold: One, being physically alive because of previously learned skills, after facing peril, two, (and to both Muir and Mummery the most important) the spiritual and mental uplift—the aesthetics of climbing which justifies the danger and risk because it is the power of risk and danger that opens new vistas not available other wise:

There is an educative and purifying power in danger that is to be found in no other school, and it is worth much for a man to know that he is not "clean gone to flesh pots and effeminacy." It may be admitted that the mountains occasionally push things a trifle too far, and bring before their votaries a vision of the imminence of dissolution that the hangman himself with all his paraphernalia of scaffold, gallows, and drop, could hardly hope to excel. But grim and hopeless as the cliffs may sometimes look when ebbing twilight is chased by shrieking wind and snow and the furies are in mad hunt along the ridges there is ever the feeling that brave companions and a constant spirit will cut the gathering web of peril.

One of the greatest blessings found in climbing is the break-down of class barriers between climbers. In climbing one's social or professional station is of little importance. Climbing allows men to come together in an arena; but, as Mummery states "in cleaner and searching sunlight, we are afoot with the quiet gods, and men can know each other and themselves for what they are" (Mummery 327).

The comradery found among climbers is based on individual strengths and limits.The only way one can contribute to the success of the group is to know where there is an asset or a liability. This is also true, not only of climbing expeditions, but is true in society. One must learn what one's limitations are, and this knowledge comes from experience and participation. This participation is not forced but seems to be innate—human beings like to test themselves—to gamble and do so knowing the possible outcome:

> The love of wager, our religious teachers notwithstanding, is still inherent in the race, and one cannot find a higher stake—at all events in these days, when Old Nick will no longer lay sterling coin against the gamester's soul—than the continuity of the cervical vertebrae; and this is the stake that the mountaineer habitually and constantly wagers. It is true the odds are all on his side, but the off-chance excites honesty of thought and tests how far decay has penetrated the inner fibre. That mountaineering has a high educational value, few, who have the requisite knowledge to

form a fair judgment, would deny. That it has its evil side I frankly admit. None can look down its gloomy deathroll without feeling that our sport demands a fearful price. (Mummery 327-328)

Yet as Mummery also states:"A man can never know his capabilities till he has tried them, and this testing process involves risk" (Mummery 331). To be a member of any group—one as small as a two-man rope or as large as that of the entire human race—there are responsibilities involved. Part of those responsibilities is the knowledge of oneself, one's assets and liabilities, and one's environment. It is this knowledge that allows humans to adapt to different situations, that has allowed him to evolve to the current pinnacle of existence. To fail to use one's ability to reason is inexcusable, as it is not only dangerous to the individual but to the group: "A man should never knowingly and deliberately thrust himself into places where he is hopelessly mastered and dominated by his environment" (Mummery 350-351).

With these factors considered: risk, challenge, limitations, experience, adaptability, Mummery's philosophy provides one of the best answers as to why men climb and he does this with a poetic quality reflective of his inner-most feelings. Such feelings call for the use of words to convey rich experience—a poetic response:

On the other hand he gains a knowledge of himself, a love of all that is most beautiful in nature, and an outlet such as no other sport affords for the stirring energies of youth; gains for which no price is, perhaps, too high. It is true the great ridges sometimes demand their sacrifice, but the mountaineer would hardly forego his worship though he knew himself to be the desired victim. But happily to most of us the great brown slabs bending over into immeasurable space, the lines and curves of the wind-molded cornice, the delicate undulations of the fissured snow, are old and trusted friends, ever luring us to health and fun and laughter, and enabling us to bid a sturdy defiance to all the ills that time and life oppose. (Mummery 352)

Annapurna, South Face. 1970

Albert Fredrick Mummery

Mountain and mountaineer.

Albert Fredrick Mummery

Works Cited

Anderson, J.R.L. *The Ulysses Factor.* New York: Harcourt Brace Jovanovich, Inc. 1970.

Begley, Martin. *"Risky Business."* **Backpacker.** May 1986: 38.

Bonatti, Walter. *The Great Days.* Trans. Geoffrey Sutton. London: Victor Gollanez Ltd, 1963.

Blum, Arlene. *Annapurna: A Woman's Place.* San Francisco: Sierra Club Books, 1980.

Conrad, Joseph. *Lord Jim.* New York: Signet, 1961.

Conrad, Joseph. *The Heart of Darkness.* New York: Signet, 1950.

Donne, John. *"Meditation XVII"* in **The Norton Anthology of English Literature** ed. Abrams, et al. New York: Norton, 1968.

Furlons, William Berry. "Doctor Danger." *Outside.* January 1981: 40-42, 92-95.

Gervasutti, Giusto. *Gervesutti's Climbs.* Trans. Nea Morin and Janet Adams Smith. Seattle: The Mountaineers, 1979.

Herzog, Maurice. *Annapurna.* Trans. Nea Morin and Janet Adams Smith. New York: E.P. Dutton & Co., Inc., 1953.

Hunt, Sir John. *The Conquest of Everest.* New York: E.P. Dutton & Co., Inc., 1954.

Irwin, William Roberts, Ed. *Challenge: An Anthology of the Literature of Mountaineering.* New York: Columbia University Press, 1973.

James, William. *Essays on Faith and Morals.* New York: Lonmans, Green and Co., 1947.

Lathem, Edward Connery, Ed. *The Poetry of Robert Frost.* New York: Holt, Rinehart and Winston, 1969.

Long, Jeff. "Cannibals." *Early Winters 10th Anniversary Catalog. 1982*: 93-97.

Muir, John. *The Mountains of California.* Berkeley: Ten Speed Press, 1977.

Mummery, A. F. *My Climbs in the Alps and Caucasus.* London: Basil Blackwell Oxford, 1946.

Neate, W. R. *Mountaineering and its Literature.* Harmony Hall, England: Cicerone Press, 1978.

Rebuffat, Gaston. *Starlight and Storm.* E.P. New York: Dutton & Company, Inc., 1957.

Roberts, David. *Mountain of My Fear "The Wilderness Reader."* ed. Frank Bergon. New York: Mentor, 1980.

Sayre, Woodrow Wilson. *Four Against Everest.* Englewood Cliffs: Prentice-Hall, Inc., 1964.

Schulthers, Rob. *The Adventurers."* **Outside.** January 1981: 33-34.

Scott, Doug. *"A Crawl Down the Ogre."* **Mountain 57.** September 1977: 38-46.

Scott, Doug. *"On the Profundity Trail."* **Mountain 15.** May 1971: 12-17.

Shelley, Mary. *Frankenstein.* London: Dent, 1973.

Shelley, Percy Bysshe. *"A Defence of Poetry"* in **English Romantic Poetry and Prose.** ed. Russell Noyes. New York: Oxford University Press, 1979.

Smith, George Alan and Carol D. Smith. *The Armchair Mountaineer.* New York: Pitman Publishing Corp., 1968.

Stephen, Leslie. *The Playground of Europe* ed. H.E.G. Tyndale, Oxford: Basil Blackwell Ltd., 1936.

Styles, Showell. *The Mountaineers Week-End Book.* London: Seeley Service and Co. LTD., 2960. *"The China Everest Expedition"*, **PBS.** October 14, 1983.

Thoreau, Henry David. *"Walking."* **The Great English and American Essays.** ed. Edmund Fuller. New York: Avon Books, 1964.

Tobias, Michael Charles, and Harold Drasado. *The Mountain Spirit.* New York: The Overlook Press, 1979.

Trollope, Anthony. *"A Further Defense"* in **Challenge: An Anthology of the Literature of Mountaineering.** ed. William Robert Irwin. New York: Columbia University Press, 1973.

Vasconcelos, Jose. *"The Boar Hunt"* in **The Realm of Fiction** ed. James B. Hall. New York: McGraw-Hill, Co., 1970.

Vetter, Craig. *"John Bachar Hangs On."* **Outside**. April 1986: 38-42, 113-117.

Wolf, Linnie Marsh, ed. ***John of the Mountains: The Unpublished Journals of John Muir***. Madison: University of Wisconsin Press, 1979.

notes:

5/7/95 - After the gun-shots ran pyronia
through me and the entire
airport spirit - I pondered how
lifes experiences often involve
curious timing... How very little
I really control everything. My
strong desire to climb seems out
of control, however the climb
itself is controlled. How I put myself
in this vertical situation is goofy,
how I get out alive or at least
unhurt is serious enough to
require 100% of my attention. Maybe
thats it - I'm forced to completely
focus or pay huge consequences.
When live safely staffy, (mentally
clip-in, tied to my life-line
that studies my up the summit
never never easy to gain, and even
when the summit is at hand, still
no immediate gratification, only
after descenting back to the foothills
does it sink in of what ive done
climbed to the top of the earth
only to gaze all around and down
120 wondering why I'm here anyway. I've
never found the answer, but continue to
seek for one. Knowing clearly my place

...s not atop a mighty mountain peak. But deep inside my soul. The terrific physical demand to summit. The exhileration. Shine 'light on my hidden notes:... The danger, the truths... But still I can not see them because I know they are there — I suppose I'm curious... So whats over the next ridge? Lets see, lets climb just once more... why not... The weather looks good.

notes:

notes:

notes:

notes:

notes:

notes:

Other Books published by Mountain N'Air Books:

The Best Day Hikes of the California Northwest

Art Bernstein
ISBN:1-879415-02-X **$13.50**
From Marin to Crescent City, to Mt. Shasta including the Trinity Alps,
Russian and Marble Wilderness Areas

Best Hikes of the Trinity Alps

Art Bernstein
ISBN: 1-879415-05-4 **$17.00**
A hiking, backpacking, natural history and lake fishing Guide to the
Northern California area, including the Trinity Alps, Yolla Bolly-Middle
Eel, Castle Crags, and Snow Mountain Wilderness Areas.

Great Rock Hits of Hueco Tanks

Paul Piana
ISBN:1-879415-03-8 **$ 6.95**
120 climbing routes to this climber's winter paradise, located near El Paso,
Texas, near the Mexican border, described by Paul Piana.

High Endeavors

Pat Ament
ISBN:1-879415-00-3 **$12.95**
Some of the best essays written by Pat Ament. A climber with passion and
vision.

Rock And Roses

Mikel Vause, editor
ISBN: 1-879415-01-1 **$11.95**
An anthology of mountaineering essays, by some of the best climbers in
the world. it includes contributions form 16 women from all walks of life.